CCNA: Cisco Certified Network Associate for Beginners

MICHAELLE CONRREDE

Table of Contents

PART I: Cisco IOS 6
   Cisco IOS overview 6
   Accessing the IOS 6
      IOS modes 7
   Power on a Cisco device 8
   IOS command modes 9
      User EXEC mode commands 9
      Privileged EXEC mode commands 10
      Global configuration mode commands 11
      Submode commands 12
   Get help in IOS 12
   Running & startup configuration 14
   IOS basic commands 15
      Hostname command 15
      No shutdown command 16
      IP address command 16
      Setting up passwords 16
      Service password-encryption command 18
      Configuring banners 18
      Show version command 19
      Show history command 20
      Show running-configuration & show startup-configuration commands
      21
   Show command 22
   Configure descriptions 23
   Run privileged commands within global config mode 24
   Ports on an IOS device 25
   Pipe character in IOS 27
   IOS boot sequence 28
   Backing up IOS configuration 29

PART II: IP Routing 32
   What is IP routing? 32
      Default gateway 32
      Routing table 33
   Connected, static & dynamic routes 34
      Connected routes 34
      Static routes 35
      Dynamic routes 37
   Administrative distance & metric 38
      Administrative distance 38
      Metric 39

2

Routing protocols 40
Types of routing protocols 40
   Distance vector protocols 41
   Link state protocols 41

PART III: RIP 44

RIP overview 44
Configuring RIPv2 45
Passive-interface command 46
RIP loop prevention 47
   Split Horizon 47
   Route poisoning 48
   Hold down timer 49
Advertise default routes using RIP 49

PART IV: EIGRP 51

EIGRP overview 51
   EIGRP Neighbors 51
   Feasible and reported distance 52
   Successor and feasible successor 53
   EIGRP topology table 54
EIGRP configuration 54
   Configuring EIGRP 1 54
   Configuring EIGRP 2 56
Wildcard mask in EIGRP 58
EIGRP automatic & manual summarization 59
   EIGRP automatic summarization 59
   EIGRP manual summarization 61
EIGRP authentication & load balancing 63
   EIGRP authentication 63
   EIGRP load balancing 64
EIGRP Reliable Transport Protocol (RTP) 66
EIGRP Diffusing Update Algorithm (DUAL) 67
EIGRP summary 67

PART V: OSPF 69

OSPF overview 69
   OSPF neighbors 69
   OSPF neighbor states 70
   OSPF areas 70
   LSA, LSU and LSR 72
OSPF configuration 73
   Configuring OSPF 1 73
   Configuring OSPF 2 74
Designated & Backup Designated Router 76
OSPF authentication 77
OSPF summarization 79

OSPF summary 81
Differences between OSPF and EIGRP 81
Comparing internal routing protocols (IGPs) 81

PART VI: LAN Switching 84

Layer 2 switching 84
    Differences between hubs and switches 85
How switches work 86
Collision & broadcast domain 89
    Collision domain 89
    Broadcast domain 89
CSMA/CD 90

PART VII: VLAN 92

What is a VLAN? 92
Access and trunk ports 93
Configuring VLANs 94
Configuring access & trunk ports 95
Frame tagging 97
IEEE 802.1Q 98
Inter-Switch Link (ISL) 99
Configuring voice VLANs 99
Configuring allowed VLANs 101

PART VIII: VTP 103

What is VTP? 103
VTP modes 104
VTP configuration 105

PART IX: NAT 108

What is NAT? 108
Static NAT 108
Dynamic NAT 109
Port Address Translation (PAT) configuration 111

PART X: IPv6 114

What is IPv6? 114
    IPv6 features 114
IPv6 address format 114
    IPv6 address shortening 115
Types of IPv6 addresses 116
IPv6 unicast addresses 116
IPv6 global unicast addresses 116
IPv6 unique local addresses 117
IPv6 link-local addresses 117
IPv6 multicast addresses 118
IPv6 address prefixes 118

IPv6 interface identifier 118
IPv6 transition options 119
IPv6 routing protocols 119
How to configure IPv6 120
RIPng 121
Differences between IPv4 and IPv6 122

PART XI: STP and RSTP 123
What is STP? 123
How STP works 124
BPDU (Bridge Protocol Data Unit) 125
Electing the Root Switch in STP 125
Selecting STP root port 127
Selecting STP designated port (DP) 128
What is RSTP? 129
How RSTP works 130
Configuring RSTP 131
What are ACLs? 132
Types of ACLs 132
Configuring standard ACLs 134
Configuring extended ACLs 136
Configuring named ACLs 139

PART I: Cisco IOS

Cisco IOS overview

IOS (Internetwork Operating System) is a multitasking operating system used on most Cisco routers and switches. IOS has a command-line interface with the predetermined number of multiple-word commands. This operating system is used to configure routing, switching, internetworking and other features supported by a Cisco device.

Below you can see how IOS looks like when a Cisco device is started for the first time:

```
be found at:
http://www.cisco.com/wwl/export/crypto/tool/stqrg.html

If you require further assistance please contact us by sending email to
export@cisco.com.

Cisco CISCO1941/K9 (revision 1.0) with 491520K/32768K bytes of memory.
Processor board ID FTX152400KS
2 Gigabit Ethernet interfaces
DRAM configuration is 64 bits wide with parity disabled.
255K bytes of non-volatile configuration memory.
249856K bytes of ATA System CompactFlash 0 (Read/Write)


         --- System Configuration Dialog ---

Continue with configuration dialog? [yes/no]: n


Press RETURN to get started!



Router>
```

Accessing the IOS

There are three most common ways to access the IOS:

1. **Console access** – this type of access is usually used to configure newly acquired devices. These devices usually don't have an IP address configured, and therefore cannot be accessed through the network. Most of the Cisco devices have a physical console port. This port can be connected to a computer using a rollover cable, a special type of cable with pins on one end reversed on the other end of the cable. The rollover cable is a serial cable, which means that you can't just plug it in an Ethernet port on your computer. You will need an adapter that converts an interface on your computer (usually a 9-pin serial interface) into RJ-45.

> NOTE
>
> Newer Cisco devices usually include a USB console port, since serial ports are rare on modern PCs.

2. **Telnet access** – this type of access used to be a common way to access network devices. Telnet is a terminal emulation program that enables you to access IOS through the network and configure the device remotely. The device that is being configured needs to have a Telnet server installed and an IP address configured.

    Telnet uses a well-known TCP port 23. One of the biggest disadvantages of this protocol is that is sends all data as clear text, which includes the passwords! This is the reason why this type of access is usually not used anymore. Instead, SSH is usually used.

3. **SSH access** – like Telnet, this access type enables you to configure devices remotely, but it adds an extra layer of security by encrypting all communications using public-key cryptography. SSH uses well known TCP port 22.

IOS modes

IOS has many different modes. There are three main modes any many submodes. We will describe the three main modes and one submode.

- User EXEC mode – the default mode for the IOS CLI. This is the mode that a user is placed in after accessing the IOS. Only basic commands (like ping or telnet) are available in this mode.
- Privileged EXEC Mode – this mode is accessed by typing the enable command from the user EXEC mode. This mode can be password protected. In this mode a user can view and change a device's configuration.
- Global configuration mode – this mode can be accessed by typing the configure terminal command from the privileged EXEC mode. It is used to change the device's configuration.

A global configuration mode can have many submodes. For example, when a user wants to configure an interface, he will have to enter the interface submode by entering the interface INTERFACE_TYPE INTERFACE_NUMBER command (e.g. interface FastEthernet 0/1) from the global configuration mode. This submode can have many commands that are specific for the interface.

Let's describe each of the modes mentioned above in more detail.

Power on a Cisco device

When you first power-on a newly purchased Cisco device, it will perform a power-on self-test (POST) to discover the hardware components and verify that all components work properly. If the POST is successful, the device will enter the setup mode. This mode presents a step-by-step dialog to help you configure some basic parameters, such as the device hostname, passwords, interface IP address, etc. To enter the setup mode, power on your device and type yes when prompted to make a selection:

```
         --- System Configuration Dialog ---

Continue with configuration dialog? [yes/no]: yes

At any point you may enter a question mark '?' for help.
Use ctrl-c to abort configuration dialog at any prompt.
Default settings are in square brackets '[]'.


Basic management setup configures only enough connectivity
for management of the system, extended setup will ask you
to configure each interface on the system

Would you like to enter basic management setup? [yes/no]: yes
Configuring global parameters:

  Enter host name [Router]: R1

  The enable secret is a password used to protect access to
  privileged EXEC and configuration modes. This password, after
  entered, becomes encrypted in the configuration.
  Enter enable secret: cisco

  The enable password is used when you do not specify an
  enable secret password, with some older software versions, and
  some boot images.
  Enter enable password: secret

  The virtual terminal password is used to protect
  access to the router over a network interface.
  Enter virtual terminal password: secret
Configure SNMP Network Management? [no]:
```

The wizard guides you through the initial configuration of your device and will create an initial configuration file. The setup mode is useful when you are unfamiliar with the IOS CLI, but once you learn the basics of CLI, you probably won't use this mode ever again.

> NOTE
>
> You can enter the setup mode at any time from the command line by typing the setup command from the privileged mode. To exit the setup mode without saving any changes, press CRTL+C.

IOS command modes

We've already learned that IOS has three main command modes: the user exec, privileged exec, and the global configuration modes. Each of these modes serves a different purpose and has its own set of commands. In this lesson we will describe each of this modes in more detail.

User EXEC mode commands

Initially, a user logs into the User Exec mode. This is the mode with the least number of commands. You can get a list of all available commands by typing the character ?.

```
Press RETURN to get started!


Router>?
Exec commands:
  <1-99>      Session number to resume
  connect     Open a terminal connection
  disable     Turn off privileged commands
  disconnect  Disconnect an existing network connection
  enable      Turn on privileged commands
  exit        Exit from the EXEC
  logout      Exit from the EXEC
  ping        Send echo messages
  resume      Resume an active network connection
  show        Show running system information
  ssh         Open a secure shell client connection
  telnet      Open a telnet connection
  terminal    Set terminal line parameters
  traceroute  Trace route to destination
Router>
Router>
```

As you can see, most of the commands available are used to show statistics and perform some basic troubleshooting. The prompt on the left side of the screen always displays the device hostname (R1 in this case), followed by the character >.

All commands can be abbreviated to their first letters of the command name. For example, you can abbreviate ping by typing pin, because no other command in the User EXEC mode IOS mode begins with these letters.

Privileged EXEC mode commands

This IOS mode is also called enable mode because you must enter the enable command from a user EXEC mode if you want to access this mode. You can use more commands in the privileged EXEC mode than you were able to use in the user EXEC mode. You can save a device configuration or reload a device in this mode. You can also enter a third mode, the configuration mode. The access to the privileged EXEC mode is usually protected with a password.

The prompt for this mode shows # after the device hostname.

```
Router>en
Router#?
Exec commands:
  <1-99>      Session number to resume
  auto        Exec level Automation
  clear       Reset functions
  clock       Manage the system clock
  configure   Enter configuration mode
  connect     Open a terminal connection
  copy        Copy from one file to another
  debug       Debugging functions (see also 'undebug')
  delete      Delete a file
  dir         List files on a filesystem
  disable     Turn off privileged commands
  disconnect  Disconnect an existing network connection
  enable      Turn on privileged commands
  erase       Erase a filesystem
  exit        Exit from the EXEC
  logout      Exit from the EXEC
  mkdir       Create new directory
  more        Display the contents of a file
  no          Disable debugging informations
  ping        Send echo messages
  reload      Halt and perform a cold restart
  resume      Resume an active network connection
  rmdir       Remove existing directory
  setup       Run the SETUP command facility
  show        Show running system information
  ssh         Open a secure shell client connection
  telnet      Open a telnet connection
  terminal    Set terminal line parameters
  traceroute  Trace route to destination
  undebug     Disable debugging functions (see also 'debug')
  vlan        Configure VLAN parameters
  write       Write running configuration to memory, network, or termi
```

Global configuration mode commands

To change a device configuration, you need to enter the global configuration mode. This mode can be accessed by typing configure terminal (or conf t, the abbreviated version of the command) from the enable mode. The prompt for this mode is hostname(config).

Global configuration mode commands are used to configure a device. You can set a hostname, configure authentication, set an IP address for an interface, etc. From this mode you can also access submodes, for example the interface mode, from where you can configure interface options.

You can get back to a privileged EXEC mode by typing the end command. You can also type CTRL + C to exit the configuration mode.

```
Router#configure terminal
Enter configuration commands, one per line.  End with CNTL/Z.
Router(config)#?
Configure commands:
  aaa                 Authentication, Authorization and Accounting.
  access-list         Add an access list entry
  banner              Define a login banner
  boot                Modify system boot parameters
  cdp                 Global CDP configuration subcommands
  class-map           Configure Class Map
  clock               Configure time-of-day clock
  config-register     Define the configuration register
  crypto              Encryption module
  do                  To run exec commands in config mode
  dot11               IEEE 802.11 config commands
  enable              Modify enable password parameters
  end                 Exit from configure mode
  exit                Exit from configure mode
  hostname            Set system's network name
  interface           Select an interface to configure
  ip                  Global IP configuration subcommands
  ipv6                Global IPv6 configuration commands
  line                Configure a terminal line
  logging             Modify message logging facilities
  login               Enable secure login checking
  mac-address-table   Configure the MAC address table
  no                  Negate a command or set its defaults
  ntp                 Configure NTP
  parser              Configure parser
  policy-map          Configure QoS Policy Map
  priority-list       Build a priority list
  privilege           Command privilege parameters
  queue-list          Build a custom queue list
  radius-server       Modify Radius query parameters
```

Submode commands

A global configuration mode contains many submodes. For example, if you want to configure an interface you have to enter that interface configuration mode. Each submode contains only commands that pertain to the resource that is being configured.

To enter the interface configuration mode you need to specify which interface you would like to configure. This is done by using the interface INTERFACE_TYPE/INTERFACE_NUMBER global configuration command, where INTERFACE_TYPE represents the type of an interface (Ethernet, FastEthernet, Serial…) and INTERFACE_NUMBER represents the interface number, since CIsco devices usually have more than one physical interface. Once inside the interface configuration mode, you can get a list of available commands by typing the "?" character. Each submode has its own prompt. Notice how the command prompt was changed to Router(config-if) after I've entered the interface submode:

```
Router(config)#int fastEthernet 0/1
Router(config-if)#?
  arp                Set arp type (arpa, probe, snap) or timeout
  bandwidth          Set bandwidth informational parameter
  cdp                CDP interface subcommands
  crypto             Encryption/Decryption commands
  custom-queue-list  Assign a custom queue list to an interface
  delay              Specify interface throughput delay
  description        Interface specific description
  duplex             Configure duplex operation.
  exit               Exit from interface configuration mode
  fair-queue         Enable Fair Queuing on an Interface
  hold-queue         Set hold queue depth
  ip                 Interface Internet Protocol config commands
  ipv6               IPv6 interface subcommands
  mac-address        Manually set interface MAC address
  mtu                Set the interface Maximum Transmission Unit (MTU)
  no                 Negate a command or set its defaults
  pppoe              pppoe interface subcommands
  priority-group     Assign a priority group to an interface
  service-policy     Configure QoS Service Policy
  shutdown           Shutdown the selected interface
  speed              Configure speed operation.
  tx-ring-limit      Configure PA level transmit ring limit
  zone-member        Apply zone name
```

Get help in IOS

You can use the question mark to display a list of commands available in the prompt you are in:

12

```
Router#
Router#?
Exec commands:
  <1-99>      Session number to resume
  auto        Exec level Automation
  clear       Reset functions
  clock       Manage the system clock
  configure   Enter configuration mode
  connect     Open a terminal connection
  copy        Copy from one file to another
  debug       Debugging functions (see also 'undebug')
  delete      Delete a file
  dir         List files on a filesystem
  disable     Turn off privileged commands
  disconnect  Disconnect an existing network connection
  enable      Turn on privileged commands
  erase       Erase a filesystem
  exit        Exit from the EXEC
  logout      Exit from the EXEC
  mkdir       Create new directory
  more        Display the contents of a file
  no          Disable debugging informations
  ping        Send echo messages
  reload      Halt and perform a cold restart
 --More--
```

If the output spans more than one page, press the spacebar to display the following page of commands, or press Enter to go one command at a time. To quit the output, press **q**.

To display only commands that start with a particular character or a string of characters, type the letters and then press the question mark:

```
Router#
Router#de?
debug  delete
```

In the picture above you can see that we've displayed all commands that start with de.

If the command is more than one word long, you can use the question mark to display the next command in a string:

```
Router#
Router#debug ?
  aaa          AAA Authentication, Authorization and Accounting
  crypto       Cryptographic subsystem
  custom-queue Custom output queueing
  eigrp        EIGRP Protocol information
  ephone       ethernet phone skinny protocol
  frame-relay  Frame Relay
  ip           IP information
  ipv6         IPv6 information
  ntp          NTP information
  ppp          PPP (Point to Point Protocol) information
Router#debug eigrp ?
  fsm          EIGRP Dual Finite State Machine events/actions
  packets      EIGRP packets
```

In the picture above you can see that we've displayed all commands that can follow the command debug. We then displayed all commands that can follow the commands **debug eigrp**.

You can also autocomplete a command. Just type the first few characters and press Tab. If there is only a single match, IOS will complete the command.

You don't have to type an entire word to finish a command. Just can type just the first letter or a couple of letters, and if there is only a single match, IOS will understand what you are trying to accomplish. For example, you can type sh ip int b instead of a longer version, show ip interface brief:

```
Router#sh ip int b
Interface             IP-Address      OK? Method Status                Protocol
FastEthernet0/0       unassigned      YES unset  administratively down down
FastEthernet0/1       unassigned      YES unset  administratively down down
Vlan1                 unassigned      YES unset  administratively down down
```

Note that we were able to execute the command above because each set of characters had only one match in the list of commands. If we've typed sh ip in b instead, IOS would not have understood our intention:

```
Router#
Router#show ip in b
% Ambiguous command: "show ip in b"
```

The % Ambiguous command: "show ip in b" message was displayed because the third keyword, in, has more than one meaning (inspect or interface).

Running & Startup configuration

Cisco devices store commands in two configuration files:

14

- Startup configuration
- Running configuration

Immediately after you type a command in the global configuration mode, it will be stored in the running configuration. A running configuration resides in a device's RAM, so if a device loses power, all configured commands will be lost.

To avoid this scenario, you need to copy your current configuration into the startup configuration. A startup configuration is stored in the nonvolatile memory of a device, which means that all configuration changes are saved even if the device loses power.

To copy your running configuration into the startup configuration you need to type the command copy running-configuration startup-configuration.

```
Router#copy running-config startup-config
Destination filename [startup-config]?
Building configuration...
[OK]
Router#
```

IOS basic commands

In this article we will go through some basic IOS commands.

Hostname command

The hostname command is used to configure the device hostname. Because this command changes a device configuration, it must be entered in the global configuration mode. After typing the command, the prompt will change and display the new hostname.

Here is an example that shows you how to change a hostname of a device.

First, enter the global configuration mode by typing the enable command in the user EXEC mode and the configuration terminal command in the privileged EXEC mode. Once inside the global configuration mode, type the command hostname R1. Notice how the prompt was changed to reflect the configured value.

```
Router>
Router>enable
Router#config
Router#configure te
Router#configure terminal
Enter configuration commands, one per line. End with CNTL/Z.
Router(config)#hostname R1
R1(config)#
```

No shutdown command

By default, all interfaces on a Cisco router are turned off. To enable an interface, the no shutdown command is used. You first need to enter the submode of the interface that you want to configure. You can do that by using the global configuration mode command interface INTERFACE_TYPE/INTERFACE_NUMBER. You can get a list of available interfaces by typing the '?' character after the interface command.

You may notice that the prompt has changed to reflect the mode you are currently in. For the interface mode the HOSTNAME#(config-if) prompt is shown.

Once inside the interface mode, you can enable an interface by typing the no shutdown command.

```
R1(config)#interface fa0/1
R1(config-if)#no shutdown

R1(config-if)#
%LINK-5-CHANGED: Interface FastEthernet0/1, changed state to up

R1(config-if)#
```

IP address command

The ip address interface mode command is used to assign an IP address to an interface. The syntax of this command is ip address IP_ADDRESS SUBNET_MASK. For example, if we want to assign an IP address of 10.0.0.1 with the subnet mask 255.0.0.0 to a interface, we would use the following command:

ip address 10.0.0.1 255.0.0.0

What if you had made a mistake and written the ip address 10.0.0.2 255.0.0.0 command instead of the command above? Well, you can remove the wrong IP address by typing the same command, but this time with the no keyword in front of it, in our case no ip address. You can remove any command from your IOS configuration by using the no keyword in front of the command.

```
Router(config-if)#ip address 10.0.0.2 255.0.0.0
Router(config-if)#no ip address
```

Setting up passwords

Each Cisco IOS device has the built-in authentication features. There are three basic ways to configure authentication on a device:

❖ Configure a password for the console access – by default, the console access doesn't require a password. You can configure a password for the console access by using the following set of commands:

```
HOSTNAME(config) line console 0
HOSTNAME(config-line) password PASSWORD
HOSTNAME(config-line) login
```

This will force a user to type the password when trying to access the device through the console port.

```
User Access Verification

Password:

Router>
```

❖ Configure a password for the telnet access – by default, the telnet access is disabled. You need to enable it. This is done using the following sequence of commands:

```
HOSTNAME(config) line vty FIRST_VTY LAST_VTY
HOSTNAME(config-line) password PASSWORD
HOSTNAME(config-line) login
```

The first command defines a range of virtual terminal sessions that you would like to configure. A virtual session can be a telnet or SSH session. Cisco devices usually supports 16 concurrent VTY sessions. So, this command usually looks like this: line vty 0 15.

The login command allows a remote access to a device. It is required in order for telnet to work.

```
PC>telnet 10.0.0.2
Trying 10.0.0.2 ...Open

User Access Verification

Password:
R1>
```

❖ Configure a password for the privileged EXEC mode – from the privileged EXEC mode you can enter the global configuration mode and change the configuration of a device. Therefore, it is important to prevent an unauthorized user from entering the global configuration mode. You can do that by setting up a password to enter the privileged EXEC mode. This can be done in two ways:

```
HOSTNAME(config) enable password PASSWORD
HOSTNAME(config) enable secret PASSWORD
```

Both of the commands above accomplish the same thing, but with one major difference. The enable secret *PASSWORD* commands encrypts the password, while the enable password *PASSWORD* command doesn't, which means that an unauthorized user could just read a password from the device configuration:

```
Building configuration...

Current configuration : 553 bytes
!
version 12.4
no service timestamps log datetime msec
no service timestamps debug datetime msec
no service password-encryption
!
hostname R1
!
!
!
enable password cisco
```

Notice how the password (cisco) is visible in the device's configuration.

Service password-encryption command

By default, passwords configured using the enable password command and passwords for the console or telnet access are stored in clear text in the configuration file. This presents a security risk because an attacker could easily find out passwords. The global configuration service password-encryption command encrypts all passwords configured.

It is important to note that this type of password encryption is not consider especially secure, since the algorithm used can be easily cracked. Cisco recommends using this command only with additional security measures.

Configuring banners

You can display a banner on a Cisco device. A banner is usually shown before the login prompt. It is usually some text that appears on the screen when a user connects to the device (e.g. some legal information).

The most commonly used banner is the Message of The Day (MOTD) banner. This banner, if configured, is shown before the login prompt to every user that is trying to establish a session with the device. The following global configuration command is used to configure a MOTD banner:

18

```
hostname(config) banner motd DELIMITING_CHARACTER TEXT
DELIMITING_CHARACTER
```

A delimiting character is a character of your choice. Its purpose is to signify the start and end of a text that will appear in the banner. For example, the command banner motd # Unauthorized access forbidden! # will show the following text: Unauthorized access forbidden!

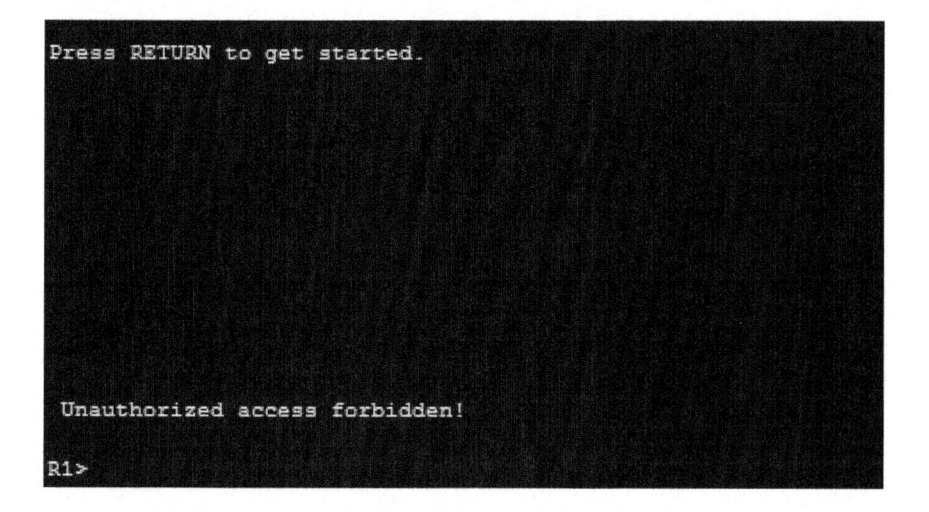

```
Press RETURN to get started.




Unauthorized access forbidden!
R1>
```

Show version command

The show version command is used to display information about a Cisco device. The command can be entered in both the user EXEC and privileged EXEC mode. By using this command you can find out many useful information about your Cisco device, such as:

- ❖ Software Version – IOS software version
- ❖ System up-time – time since last reboot
- ❖ Software image name – IOS filename stored in flash
- ❖ Hardware Interfaces – interfaces available on device
- ❖ Configuration Register value – bootup specifications, console speed setting, etc.
- ❖ Amount of RAM memory – amount of RAM memory
- ❖ Amount of NVRAM memory
- ❖ Amount of Flash memory

The following example shows the output of the command:

```
R1>show version
Cisco IOS Software, 1841 Software (C1841-ADVIPSERVICESK9-M), Version 12.4(15)T1,
 RELEASE SOFTWARE (fc2)
Technical Support: http://www.cisco.com/techsupport
Copyright (c) 1986-2007 by Cisco Systems, Inc.
Compiled Wed 18-Jul-07 04:52 by pt_team

ROM: System Bootstrap, Version 12.3(8r)T8, RELEASE SOFTWARE (fc1)

System returned to ROM by power-on
System image file is "flash:c1841-advipservicesk9-mz.124-15.T1.bin"


This product contains cryptographic features and is subject to United
States and local country laws governing import, export, transfer and
use. Delivery of Cisco cryptographic products does not imply
third-party authority to import, export, distribute or use encryption.
Importers, exporters, distributors and users are responsible for
compliance with U.S. and local country laws. By using this product you
agree to comply with applicable laws and regulations. If you are unable
to comply with U.S. and local laws, return this product immediately.

A summary of U.S. laws governing Cisco cryptographic products may be found at:
http://www.cisco.com/wwl/export/crypto/tool/stqrg.html

If you require further assistance please contact us by sending email to
export@cisco.com.

Cisco 1841 (revision 5.0) with 114688K/16384K bytes of memory.
Processor board ID FTX0947Z18E
M860 processor: part number 0, mask 49
2 FastEthernet/IEEE 802.3 interface(s)
191K bytes of NVRAM.
63488K bytes of ATA CompactFlash (Read/Write)

Configuration register is 0x2102
```

Show history command

An IOS device stores, by default, 10 last commands you have entered in your current EXEC session. You can use the show history command from the user EXEC or privileged EXEC mode to display them.

```
R1#show history
  show version
  show history
  conf t
  en
  conf t
  show history
R1#
```

You can set a number of command saved in the buffer for the current terminal session by using the terminal history size NUMBER command from the user EXEC or privileged EXEC mode.

> NOTE
>
> Another way to recall your command from the history buffer is by using the up arrow key on your keyboard. Most recent command is recalled first.

Show running-configuration & show startup-configuration commands

After you have changed the configuration of your device you can verify its configuration. To display the current configuration, type show running-configuration from the privileged EXEC mode. This show the configuration that is stored in a device's RAM.

```
Router#show running-config
Building configuration...

Current configuration : 474 bytes
!
version 12.4
no service timestamps log datetime msec
no service timestamps debug datetime msec
no service password-encryption
!
hostname Router
!
!
!
!
!
!
!
!
!
!
!
!
spanning-tree mode pvst
!
!
!
!
interface FastEthernet0/0
 no ip address
 duplex auto
 speed auto
 shutdown
```

After you have stored your running configuration into the startup configuration, you can view the saved configuration using the show startup-config command from the privileged EXEC mode.

This command shows the configuration that is currently stored in the device's NVRAM. This configuration will be loaded next time the device is restarted.

```
Router#show startup-config
Using 474 bytes
!
version 12.4
no service timestamps log datetime msec
no service timestamps debug datetime msec
no service password-encryption
!
hostname Router
!
!
!
!
!
!
!
!
!
!
!
!
spanning-tree mode pvst
!
!
!
!
interface FastEthernet0/0
 no ip address
 duplex auto
 speed auto
 shutdown
```

Show command

We've already mentioned a couple of show commands in the previous sections, so you should already we somewhat aware of this command. This command is used to display the device's configuration, statistics, command history, interface status… The show command is invoked from the enable mode and can accept a lot of parameters:

22

```
Floor1#show ?
aaa Show AAA values
access-lists List access lists
arp Arp table
cdp CDP information
class-map Show QoS Class Map
clock Display the system clock
controllers Interface controllers status
crypto Encryption module
debugging State of each debugging option
dhcp Dynamic Host Configuration Protocol status
dot11 IEEE 802.11 show information
file Show filesystem information
flash: display information about flash: file system
…
terminal Display terminal configuration parameters
users Display information about terminal lines
version System hardware and software status
vlan-switch VTP VLAN status
vtp Configure VLAN database
```

Here is a brief description of the most popular show commands:

- show running-config – displays the running (current) configuration of your device:
- show startup-config – displays the startup configuration of your device:
- show ip interface brief – provides information about the interfaces on a router, including the logical (IP) address and status:
- show history – shows the command history:
- show interface INTERFACE – displays the status of the specified interface:
- show version – shows information about the device, such as the IOS version running on the device, number of interfaces, device model, time of the last reboot, amount of memory available on the device, etc.

Configure descriptions

Adding a description to an interface on a Cisco device doesn't provide any extra functionality, but it is useful for administrative purposes, since it will help you to remember the interface function. A description of an interface is locally significant and can be up to 240 characters long. It can be set using the description command from the interface submode:

```
DEVICE(config) interface Fa0/1
DEVICE(config-if) description WAN to London
```

Example configuration:

```
HQ_Router(config)#int Fa0/1
HQ_Router(config-if)#description WAN to London
HQ_Router(config-if)#
```

The description is displayed in the output of the show running-config command:

```
!
interface FastEthernet0/0
 no ip address
 duplex auto
 speed auto
 shutdown
!
interface FastEthernet0/1
 description WAN to London
 no ip address
 duplex auto
 speed auto
 shutdown
!
interface Vlan1
 no ip address
 shutdown
!
```

To erase the description, use the no description interface mode command (or the shortcut no desc):

```
HQ_Router(config)#int fa0/1
HQ_Router(config-if)#no desc
HQ_Router(config-if)#
```

Run privileged commands within global config mode

Beginning with the IOS 12.3, the privileged-exec mode commands (such as show running-configuration, show interface status, etc.) can be executed within the global configuration mode and its submodes. This allows you to execute privileged-exec mode commands without needing to exit the current configuration mode. Here is an example that explains the usefulness of this feature:

```
HQ_Router(config)#int fa0/1
HQ_Router(config-if)#show interface Fa0/1
                    ^
% Invalid input detected at '^' marker.

HQ_Router(config-if)#
```

In the example above you can see that we're currently in the interface submode. We want to get more information about the interface with the show interface Fa0/1 command, but we got an error because the command is not available in this mode. However, if we use the do keyword in front of the command, the command will succeed:

```
HQ_Router(config-if)#do show interface fa0/1
FastEthernet0/1 is administratively down, line protocol is down (disabled)
  Hardware is Lance, address is 0002.16c4.5302 (bia 0002.16c4.5302)
  MTU 1500 bytes, BW 100000 Kbit, DLY 100 usec,
     reliability 255/255, txload 1/255, rxload 1/255
  Encapsulation ARPA, loopback not set
  ARP type: ARPA, ARP Timeout 04:00:00,
  Last input 00:00:08, output 00:00:05, output hang never
  Last clearing of "show interface" counters never
  Input queue: 0/75/0 (size/max/drops); Total output drops: 0
  Queueing strategy: fifo
  Output queue :0/40 (size/max)
  5 minute input rate 0 bits/sec, 0 packets/sec
  5 minute output rate 0 bits/sec, 0 packets/sec
     0 packets input, 0 bytes, 0 no buffer
     Received 0 broadcasts, 0 runts, 0 giants, 0 throttles
     0 input errors, 0 CRC, 0 frame, 0 overrun, 0 ignored, 0 abort
     0 input packets with dribble condition detected
     0 packets output, 0 bytes, 0 underruns
     0 output errors, 0 collisions, 1 interface resets
     0 babbles, 0 late collision, 0 deferred
     0 lost carrier, 0 no carrier
     0 output buffer failures, 0 output buffers swapped out
HQ_Router(config-if)#
```

The command was now executed because of the do keyword. Notice that we're still in the interface submode and we can continue with the interface configuration.

Ports on an IOS device

Cisco uses the term interface to refer to physical ports on an IOS device. Interfaces can be configured with different settings, depending on the type of the interface and whether you are configuring an interface on a router or on a switch. For example, the Cisco 7201 Router has four GE physical ports (image source: Cisco):

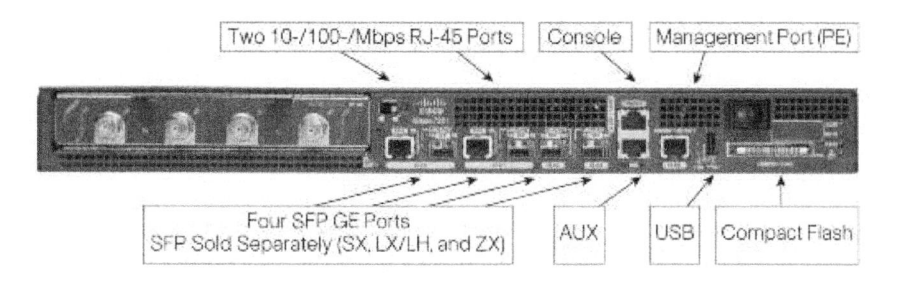

To display the router interfaces in IOS, use the show ip int brief command from the privileged exec mode:

25

```
HQ_Router#show ip int brief
Interface              IP-Address      OK? Method Status                Protocol

FastEthernet0/0        192.168.4.20    YES manual up                    up

FastEthernet0/1        unassigned      YES unset  administratively down down

Vlan1                  unassigned      YES unset  administratively down down
```

In the output above we can see that this router has 2 physical interfaces – FastEthernet0/0 and FastEthernet0/1.

Consider the output for the Fa0/0 interface:

```
HQ_Router#show ip int brief
Interface              IP-Address      OK? Method Status                Protocol

FastEthernet0/0        192.168.4.20    YES manual up                    up
```

Here is a brief description of each column:

- ❖ Interface – displays the type of the interface, in this case Fast Ethernet 0/0. The first zero specifies the physical slot on the router, while the second zero specifies the port number.
- ❖ IP-Address – displays the interface's IP address.
- ❖ OK? – YES in this column signifies that the IP address is currently valid.
- ❖ Method – manual in this column means that the interface has been manually configured. DHCP means that the interface has been configured using DHCP.
- ❖ Status – up indicates that the interface is administratively up.
- ❖ Protocol – up indicates that the interface is operational.

To configure a specific interface, use the interface TYPE SLOT/PORT command from the global config mode. This puts us in the interface submode, where we can configure various interface options:

```
HQ_Router(config)#
HQ_Router(config)#interface Fa0/0
HQ_Router(config-if)#speed 100
```

In the example above you can see that we've configured the speed option for the interface Fast Ethernet 0/0.

By default, all ports on a Cisco switch are up and running as soon as you power-on the device. This means that all you need is to connect your devices and the switch and you are good to go. This isn't the case with Cisco routers, however. You need to manually enable each interface on a router with the no shutdown interface mode command:

```
HQ_Router(config-if)#no shutdown
HQ_Router(config-if)#
%LINK-5-CHANGED: Interface FastEthernet0/0, changed state to up

%LINEPROTO-5-UPDOWN: Line protocol on Interface FastEthernet0/0, changed state to up
```

Pipe character in IOS

IOS supports the use of the pipe character (represented with the | character) to filter the output of the show and more commands. The pipe function takes the output of the command and sends it to another function, such as begin or include. This way, you can filter the output to find the section of the output that interests you. Here are a couple of examples:

```
R1#show running-config | begin interface
interface FastEthernet0/0
 no ip address
 shutdown
 duplex auto
 speed auto
!
interface FastEthernet0/1
 no ip address
 shutdown
 duplex auto
 speed auto
!
interface FastEthernet1/0
 no ip address
 shutdown
 duplex auto
 speed auto
!
interface Serial2/0
 no ip address
 shutdown
 serial restart-delay 0
!
```

In the picture above you can see that we've entered the show running-config | begin interface command. This command starts the output from the first occurrence of the word interface.

Another example, this time with include:

27

```
R1#show running-config | include password
no service password-encryption
enable password cisco
 password secret
R1#
```

As you can see from the example above, the include function displays only lines that include the word password.

To display only the section of the output about a certain feature, use the section function:

```
R1#show running-config | section vty
line vty 0 4
 password secret
 login
line vty 5 15
 password secret
 login
R1#
```

You can see in the example above that the command displayed only the vty section of the running configuration.

> NOTE
>
> Cisco Packet Tracer doesn't support the pipe function. The examples above were created in GNS3.

IOS boot sequence

The IOS boot sequence is a process performed after a Cisco IOS device is powered on. The IOS device performs a power-on self-test (POST) to test its hardware components and choose an IOS image to load. The boot sequence consists of the following steps:

1. The device performs the power-on self-test (POST) process to discover and verify its hardware components.

2. If the POST test is successful, the bootstrap program is copied from ROM into RAM.

3. The bootstrap program decides which IOS image to load from the flash memory into RAM, and then loads the chosen IOS.

Backing up IOS configuration

It is always a good idea to have a backup copy of the configuration of your IOS device. IOS configurations are usually copied to a TFTP server using the copy command. You can backup both the startup configuration and the running configuration of your device. The copy commands accept two parameters: the first parameter is the from location, and the second it the to location.

TFTP is a client-server network protocol used to send and receive files. To backup files to a TFTP server, you will have to set it up first. You can use the Packet Tracer to do so; just add a Server to your topology, assign it an IP address and enable the TFTP service:

![Server0 TFTP services configuration window showing HTTP, DHCP, DHCPv6, TFTP, DNS, SYSLOG, AAA, NTP, EMAIL, FTP services with TFTP service On and files: HQ_Router-confg, asa842-k8.bin, c1841-advipservicesk9-mz.124-15.T1.bin, c1841-ipbase-mz.123-14.T7.bin, c1841-ipbasek9-mz.124-12.bin]

To backup the startup configuration to a TFTP server, you can use the copy startup-config tftp: command:

```
HQ_Router#copy startup-config tftp:
Address or name of remote host []? 10.0.0.6
Destination filename [HQ_Router-confg]?

Writing startup-config....!!
[OK - 745 bytes]

745 bytes copied in 0.001 secs (745000 bytes/sec)
```

Remember, the first parameter after the copy keyword is the from location, while the second one is the to location. In our case, the from location is the current startup-config, and the to location is the remote TFTP server.

To restore the configuration, just switch the order of the parameters – copy tftp startup-config:

```
HQ_Router#copy tftp: startup-config
Address or name of remote host []? 10.0.0.6
Source filename []? HQ_Router-confg
Destination filename [startup-config]?

Accessing tftp://10.0.0.6/HQ_Router-confg...
Loading HQ_Router-confg from 10.0.0.6: !
[OK - 745 bytes]

745 bytes copied in 0 secs
```

Notice that we had to specify the filename, along with the IP address of the TFTP server.

PART II
IP ROUTING

PART II: IP Routing

What is IP routing?

IP routing is the process of sending packets from a host on one network to another host on a different remote network. This process is usually done by routers. Routers examine the destination IP address of a packet, determine the next-hop address, and forward the packet. Routers use routing tables to determine the next hop address to which the packet should be forwarded.

Consider the following example of IP routing:

Host A wants to communicate with host B, but host B is on another network. Host A is configured to send all packets destined for remote networks to router R1. Router R1 receives the packets, examines the destination IP address, and forwards the packet to the outgoing interface associated with the destination network.

Default gateway

A default gateway is a router that hosts use to communicate with other hosts on remote networks. A default gateway is used when a host doesn't have a route entry for the specific remote network and doesn't know how to reach that network. Hosts can be configured to send all packets destined to remote networks to the default gateway, which has a route to reach that network.

The following example explains the concept of a default gateway more thoroughly.

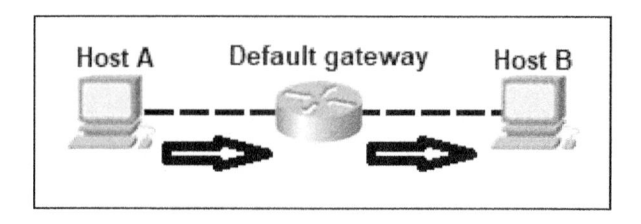

Host A has an IP address of the router R1 configured as the default gateway address. Host A is trying to communicate with host B, a host on another, remote network. Host A looks up in its routing table to check if there is an entry for that destination network. If the entry is not found, the host sends all data to the router R1. Router R1 receives the packets and forwards them to host B.

Routing table

Each router maintains a routing table and stores it in RAM. A routing table is used by routers to determine the path to the destination network. Each routing table consists of the following entries:

- network destination and subnet mask – specifies a range of IP addresses.
- remote router – IP address of the router used to reach that network.
- outgoing interface – outgoing interface the packet should go out to reach the destination network.

There are three different methods for populating a routing table:

- directly connected subnets
- using static routing
- using dynamic routing

Each of this method will be described in the following chapters.

Consider the following example. Host A wants to communicate with host B, but host B is on another network. Host A is configured to send all packets destined for remote networks to the router. The router receives the packets, checks the routing table to see if it has an entry for the destination address. If it does, the router forwards the packet out the appropriate interface port. If the router doesn't find the entry, it discards the packet.

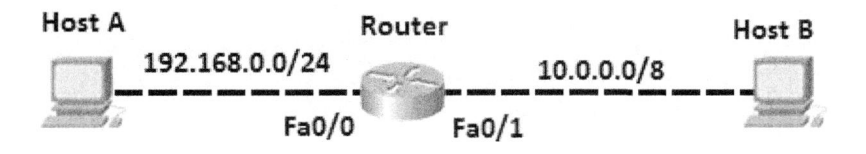

```
Host A                    Router                        Host B
      192.168.0.0/24                  10.0.0.0/8
                        Fa0/0      Fa0/1
```

We can use the show ip route command from the enabled mode to display the router's routing table.

```
Router#show ip route
Codes: C - connected, S - static, I - IGRP, R - RIP, M - mobile, B - BGP
       D - EIGRP, EX - EIGRP external, O - OSPF, IA - OSPF inter area
       N1 - OSPF NSSA external type 1, N2 - OSPF NSSA external type 2
       E1 - OSPF external type 1, E2 - OSPF external type 2, E - EGP
       i - IS-IS, L1 - IS-IS level-1, L2 - IS-IS level-2, ia - IS-IS inter area
       * - candidate default, U - per-user static route, o - ODR
       P - periodic downloaded static route

Gateway of last resort is not set

C    10.0.0.0/8 is directly connected, FastEthernet0/1
C    192.168.0.0/24 is directly connected, FastEthernet0/0
Router#
```

As you can see from the output above, this router has two directly connected routes to the subnets 10.0.0.0/8 and 192.168.0.0/24. The character C in the routing table indicates that a route is a directly connected route. So, when host A sends the packet to host B, the router will look up into its routing table and find the route to the 10.0.0.0/8 network on which host B resides. The router will then use that route to route packets received from host A to host B.

Connected, static & dynamic routes

Let's explain the types of routes that can be found in a router's routing table.

Connected routes

Subnets directly connected to a router's interface are added to the router's routing table. Interface must have an IP address configured and both interface status codes must be in the up and up state. A router will be able to route all packets destined for all hosts in subnets directly connected to its active interfaces.

Consider the following example. The router has two active interfaces, Fa0/0 and Fa0/1. Each interface has been configured with an IP address and is currently in the up-up state, so the router adds these subnets to its routing table.

```
Router#show ip route
Codes: C - connected, S - static, I - IGRP, R - RIP, M - mobile, B - BGP
       D - EIGRP, EX - EIGRP external, O - OSPF, IA - OSPF inter area
       N1 - OSPF NSSA external type 1, N2 - OSPF NSSA external type 2
       E1 - OSPF external type 1, E2 - OSPF external type 2, E - EGP
       i - IS-IS, L1 - IS-IS level-1, L2 - IS-IS level-2, ia - IS-IS inter area
       * - candidate default, U - per-user static route, o - ODR
       P - periodic downloaded static route

Gateway of last resort is not set

C    10.0.0.0/8 is directly connected, FastEthernet0/1
C    192.168.0.0/24 is directly connected, FastEthernet0/0
Router#
Router#
```

As you can see from the output above, the router has two directly connected routes to the subnets 10.0.0.0/8 and 192.168.0.0/24. The character C in the routing table indicates that a route is a directly connected route.

> NOTE
>
> You can see only connected routes in a router's routing table by typing the show ip route connected command.

Static routes

By adding static routes, a router can learn a route to a remote network that is not directly connected to one of its interfaces. Static routes are configured manually by typing the global configuration mode command ip route DESTINATION_NETWORK SUBNET_MASK NEXT_HOP_IP_ADDRESS. This type of configuration is usually used in smaller networks because of scalability reasons (you must configure each route on each router).

A simple example will help you understand the concept of static routes.

Router A ———— 192.168.0.0/24 ———— Router B ———— 10.0.1.0/24 ———— Host

Router A is directly connected to router B. Router B is directly connected to the subnet 10.0.1.0/24. Since that subnet is not directly connected to Router A, the router doesn't know how to route packets destined for that subnet. However, you can configure that route manually on router A.

35

First, consider the router A's routing table before we add the static route:

```
Router#show ip route
Codes: C - connected, S - static, I - IGRP, R - RIP, M - mobile, B - BGP
       D - EIGRP, EX - EIGRP external, O - OSPF, IA - OSPF inter area
       N1 - OSPF NSSA external type 1, N2 - OSPF NSSA external type 2
       E1 - OSPF external type 1, E2 - OSPF external type 2, E - EGP
       i - IS-IS, L1 - IS-IS level-1, L2 - IS-IS level-2, ia - IS-IS inter area
       * - candidate default, U - per-user static route, o - ODR
       P - periodic downloaded static route

Gateway of last resort is not set

C    192.168.0.0/24 is directly connected, FastEthernet0/0
```

Now, we'll use the static route command to configure router A to reach the subnet 10.0.0.0/24. The router now has the route to reach the subnet.

```
Router#conf t
Enter configuration commands, one per line. End with CNTL/Z.
Router(config)#ip route 10.0.0.0 255.255.255.0 192.168.0.2
Router(config)#exit
Router#
%SYS-5-CONFIG_I: Configured from console by console

Router#show ip route
Codes: C - connected, S - static, I - IGRP, R - RIP, M - mobile, B - BGP
       D - EIGRP, EX - EIGRP external, O - OSPF, IA - OSPF inter area
       N1 - OSPF NSSA external type 1, N2 - OSPF NSSA external type 2
       E1 - OSPF external type 1, E2 - OSPF external type 2, E - EGP
       i - IS-IS, L1 - IS-IS level-1, L2 - IS-IS level-2, ia - IS-IS inter area
       * - candidate default, U - per-user static route, o - ODR
       P - periodic downloaded static route

Gateway of last resort is not set

     10.0.0.0/24 is subnetted, 1 subnets
S       10.0.0.0 [1/0] via 192.168.0.2
C    192.168.0.0/24 is directly connected, FastEthernet0/0
```

The character S in the routing table indicates that a route is a statically configured route.

Another version of the ip route command exists. You don't have to specify the next-hop IP address. You can rather specify the exit interface of the local router. In the example above we could have typed the ip route DEST_NETWORK NEXT_HOP_INTERFACE command to instruct router A to send all traffic destined for the subnet out the right interface. In our case, the command would be ip route 10.0.0.0 255.255.255.0 Fa0/0.

Dynamic routes

A router can learn dynamic routes if a routing protocol is enabled. A routing protocol is used by routers to exchange routing information with each other. Every router in the network can then use information to build its routing table. A routing protocol can dynamically choose a different route if a link goes down, so this type of routing is fault-tolerant. Also, unlike with static routing, there is no need to manually configure every route on every router, which greatly reduces the administrative overhead. You only need to define which routes will be advertised on a router that connect directly to the corresponding subnets – routing protocols take care of the rest.

The disadvantage of dynamic routing is that it increases memory and CPU usage on a router because every router must process received routing information and calculate its routing table.

To better understand the advantages that dynamic routing protocols bring, consider the following example:

```
Router A                    Router B                    Host
         192.168.0.0/24              10.0.1.0/24
```

Both routers are running a routing protocol, namely EIGRP. There are no static routes on Router A, so R1 doesn't know how to reach the subnet 10.0.0.0/24 that is directly connected to Router B. Router B then advertises the subnet to Router A using EIGRP. Now Router A has the route to reach the subnet. This can be verified by typing the show ip route command:

```
Router_A#show ip route
Codes: C - connected, S - static, I - IGRP, R - RIP, M - mobile, B - BGP
       D - EIGRP, EX - EIGRP external, O - OSPF, IA - OSPF inter area
       N1 - OSPF NSSA external type 1, N2 - OSPF NSSA external type 2
       E1 - OSPF external type 1, E2 - OSPF external type 2, E - EGP
       i - IS-IS, L1 - IS-IS level-1, L2 - IS-IS level-2, ia - IS-IS inter area
       * - candidate default, U - per-user static route, o - ODR
       P - periodic downloaded static route

Gateway of last resort is not set

     10.0.0.0/24 is subnetted, 1 subnets
D       10.0.0.0 [90/30720] via 192.168.0.2, 00:00:09, FastEthernet0/0
C    192.168.0.0/24 is directly connected, FastEthernet0/0
Router_A#
```

You can see that Router A has learned the subnet from EIGRP. The letter D in front of the route indicates that the route has been learned through EIGRP. If the subnet 10.0.0.0/24 fails, Router B can immediately inform Router A that the subnet is no longer reachable.

Administrative distance & metric

Administrative distance

A network can use more than one routing protocol, and routers on the network can learn about a route from multiple sources. Routers need to find a way to select a better path when there are multiple paths available. Administrative distance number is used by routers to find out which route is better (lower number is better). For example, if the same route is learned from RIP and EIGRP, a Cisco router will choose the EIGRP route and stores it in the routing table. This is because EIGRP routes have (by default) the administrative distance of 90, while RIP route has a higher administrative distance of 120.

You can display the administrative distance of all routes on your router by typing the show ip route command:

```
Router_A#show ip route
Codes: C - connected, S - static, I - IGRP, R - RIP, M - mobile, B - BGP
       D - EIGRP, EX - EIGRP external, O - OSPF, IA - OSPF inter area
       N1 - OSPF NSSA external type 1, N2 - OSPF NSSA external type 2
       E1 - OSPF external type 1, E2 - OSPF external type 2, E - EGP
       i - IS-IS, L1 - IS-IS level-1, L2 - IS-IS level-2, ia - IS-IS inter area
       * - candidate default, U - per-user static route, o - ODR
       P - periodic downloaded static route

Gateway of last resort is not set

     10.0.0.0/24 is subnetted, 1 subnets
D       10.0.0.0 [90/30720] via 192.168.0.2, 00:00:09, FastEthernet0/0
C    192.168.0.0/24 is directly connected, FastEthernet0/0
Router_A#
```

In the case above, the router has only a single route in its routing table learned from a dynamic routing protocol – the EIGRP route.

The following table lists the administrative distance default values:

38

Routing Protocol	Administrative Distance
Directly connected	0
Static route	1
Internal EIGRP	90
OSPF	110
RIP	120
External EIGRP	170
Unknown	255

Metric

If a router learns two different paths for the same network from the same routing protocol, it must decide which route is better and will be placed in the routing table. Metric is the measure used to decide which route is better (lower number is better). Each routing protocol uses its own metric. For example, RIP uses hop counts as a metric, while OSPF uses cost.

The following example explains the way RIP calculates its metric and why it chooses one path over another.

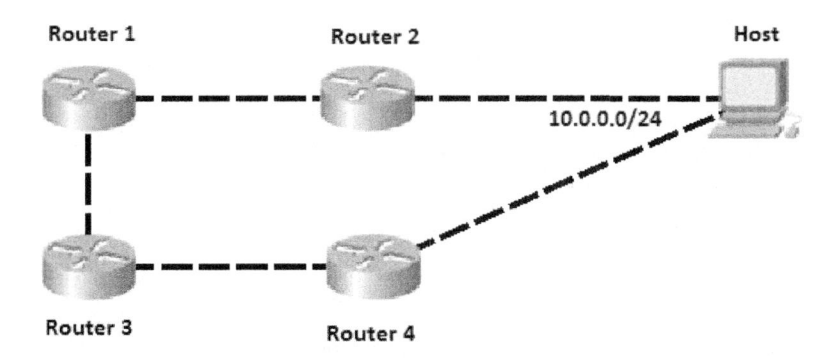

RIP has been configured on all routers. Router 1 has two paths to reach the subnet 10.0.0.0/24. One path is going through Router 2, while the other path goes through Router 3 and then Router 4. Because RIP uses the hop count as its metric, the path through Router 1 will be used to reach the 10.0.0.0/24 subnet. This is because that subnet is only one router away on the path. The other path will have a higher metric of 2, because the subnet is two routers away.

> NOTE
>
> The example above can be used to illustrate a disadvantage of using RIP as a routing protocol. Imagine if the first path through R2 was the 56k modem link, while the other path (R3-R4) is a high-speed WAN link. Router R1 would still choose the path through R2 as the best route, because RIP uses only the hop count as its metric.

The following table lists the parameters that various routing protocols use to calculate the metric:

Routing Protocol	Metric
RIP	hop count
EIGRP	bandwidth, delay
OSPF	cost

Routing protocols

Dynamic routes are routes learned via routing protocols. Routing protocols are configured on routers with the purpose of exchanging routing information. There are many benefits of using routing protocols in your network, such as:

- ❖ Unlike static routing, you don't need to manually configure every route on each router in the network. You just need to configure the networks to be advertised on a router directly connected to them.
- ❖ If a link fails and the network topology changes, routers can advertise that some routes have failed and pick a new route to that network.

Types of routing protocols

There are two types of routing protocols:

Cisco has created its own routing protocol – EIGRP. EIGRP is considered to be an advanced distance vector protocol, although some materials erroneously state that EIGRP is a hybrid routing protocol, a combination of distance vector and link state.

All of the routing protocols mentioned above are interior routing protocols (IGP), which means that they are used to exchange routing information within one autonomous system. BGP (Border Gateway Protocol) is an example of an exterior routing protocol (EGP) which is used to exchange routing information between autonomous systems on the Internet.

Distance vector protocols

As the name implies, distance vector routing protocols use distance to determine the best path to a remote network. The distance is something like the number of hops (routers) to the destination network.

Distance vector protocols usually send the complete routing table to each neighbor (a neighbor is directly connected router that runs the same routing protocol). They employ some version of Bellman-Ford algorithm to calculate the best routes. Compared with link state routing protocols, distance vector protocols are easier to configure and require little management but are susceptible to routing loops and converge slower than the link state routing protocols. Distance vector protocols also use more bandwidth because they send complete routing table, while the link state protocols send specific updates only when topology changes occur.

RIP and EIGRP are examples of distance vector routing protocols.

Link state protocols

Link state routing protocols are the second type of routing protocols. They have the same basic purpose as distance vector protocols, to find a best path to a destination, but use different methods to do so. Unlike distance vector protocols, link state protocols don't advertise the entire routing table. Instead, they advertise information about a network topology (directly connected links, neighboring routers...), so that in the end all routers running a link state protocol have the same topology database. Link state routing protocols converge much faster than distance vector routing protocols, support classless routing, send updates using multicast addresses and use triggered routing updates. They also require more router CPU and memory usage than distance-vector routing protocols and can be harder to configure.

Each router running a link state routing protocol creates three different tables:

- ❖ Neighbor table – the table of neighboring routers running the same link state routing protocol.
- ❖ Topology table – the table that stores the topology of the entire network.
- ❖ Routing table – the table that stores the best routes.

Shortest Path First algorithm is used to calculate the best route. OSPF and IS-IS are examples of link state routing protocols

Difference between distance vector and link state routing protocols

The following table summarizes the differences:

41

Distance vector	Link state
sends the entire routing table	sends only link state information
slow convergence	fast convergence
susceptible to routing loops	less susceptible to routing loops
updates are sometimes sent using broadcast	always uses multicast for the routing updates
doesn't know the network topology	knows the entire network topology
simpler to configure	can be harder to configure
examples: RIP, IGRP	examples: OSPF, IS-IS

PART III
RIP

PART III: RIP

RIP overview

RIP (Routing Information Protocol) is one of the oldest distance vector routing protocols. It is usually used on small networks because it is very simple to configure and maintain but lacks some advanced features of routing protocols like OSPF or EIGRP. Two versions of the protocol exist: version 1 and version 2. Both versions use hop count as a metric and have the administrative distance of 120. RIP version 2 is capable of advertising subnet masks and uses multicast to send routing updates, while version 1 doesn't advertise subnet masks and uses broadcast for updates. Version 2 is backwards compatible with version 1.

RIPv2 sends the entire routing table every 30 seconds, which can consume a lot of bandwidth. RIPv2 uses multicast address of 224.0.0.9 to send routing updates, supports authentication and triggered updates (updates that are sent when a change in the network occurs).

For example of how RIP works, consider the following figure.

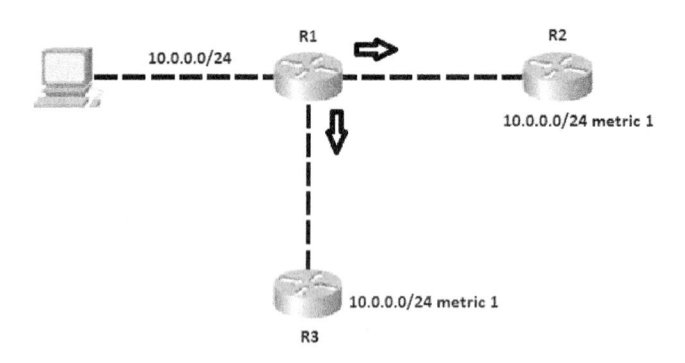

Router R1 directly connects to the subnet 10.0.0.0/24. Network engineer has configured RIP on R1 to advertise the route to this subnet. R1 sends routing updates to R2 and R3. The routing updates list the subnet, subnet mask and metric for this route. Each router, R2 and R3, receives this update and adds the route to their respective routing tables. Both routers list the metric of 1 because the network is only one hop away.

> NOTE
>
> Maximum hop count for a RIP route is 15. Any route with a higher hop count is considered to be unreachable.

Configuring RIPv2

Configuring RIPv2 is a pretty straightforward process. Only three steps are required:

The first two commands are easy to comprehend, but the last command requires a little bit more thought. With the network command you specify which interfaces will participate in the routing process. This command takes a classful network as a parameter and enables RIP on the corresponding interfaces. Let's configure our sample network to use RIP.

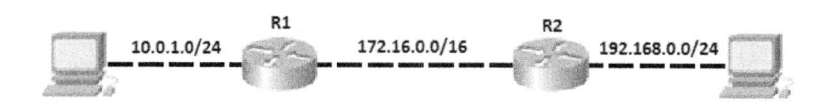

```
        R1                    R2
10.0.1.0/24    172.16.0.0/16    192.168.0.0/24
```

Router R1 and R2 have directly connected subnets. We want to include these subnets in the RIP routing process. To do that, we first need to enable RIP on both routers and then advertise these subnets using the network command.

On router R1, in the global configuration mode, enter the router rip command to enable RIP. In the RIP configuration mode, change the version of the protocol to 2 by using the version 2 command. Next, use the network 10.0.0.0 command to include the Fa0/1 interface on the router R1 in the routing process. Remember, the network command takes a classful network number as a parameter, so in this case every interface that has an IP address that begins with 10 will be included in the RIP process (IP addresses that begins with 10 are, by default, the class A addresses and have the default subnet mask of 255.0.0.0). For instance, if another interface on the router had the IP address of 10.1.0.1 it would also be included in the routing process with the network command. You also need to include the link between the two routers in the RIP routing process. This is done by adding another network statement, network 172.16.0.0.

So, the configuration on R1 should look like this:

```
R1(config)#router rip
R1(config-router)#version 2
R1(config-router)#network 10.0.0.0
R1(config-router)#network 172.16.0.0
R1(config-router)#
```

The configuration on R2 looks similar, but with different network number for the directly connected subnet:

```
R2(config)#router rip
R2(config-router)#version 2
R2(config-router)#network 192.168.0.0
R2(config-router)#network 172.16.0.0
R2(config-router)#
```

You can verify that router R1 have a route to the R2's directly connected subnet by typing the show ip route command:

```
R1#show ip route
Codes: C - connected, S - static, I - IGRP, R - RIP, M - mobile, B - BGP
       D - EIGRP, EX - EIGRP external, O - OSPF, IA - OSPF inter area
       N1 - OSPF NSSA external type 1, N2 - OSPF NSSA external type 2
       E1 - OSPF external type 1, E2 - OSPF external type 2, E - EGP
       i - IS-IS, L1 - IS-IS level-1, L2 - IS-IS level-2, ia - IS-IS inter area
       * - candidate default, U - per-user static route, o - ODR
       P - periodic downloaded static route

Gateway of last resort is not set

     10.0.0.0/24 is subnetted, 1 subnets
C       10.0.1.0 is directly connected, FastEthernet0/0
C    172.16.0.0/16 is directly connected, FastEthernet0/1
R    192.168.0.0/24 [120/1] via 172.16.0.2, 00:00:25, FastEthernet0/1
R1#
```

The legend lists R for all RIP routes in the routing table. Also note that the administrative distance of 120 is shown, together with the metric of 1.

Passive-interface command

Consider the following example network with RIP turned on:

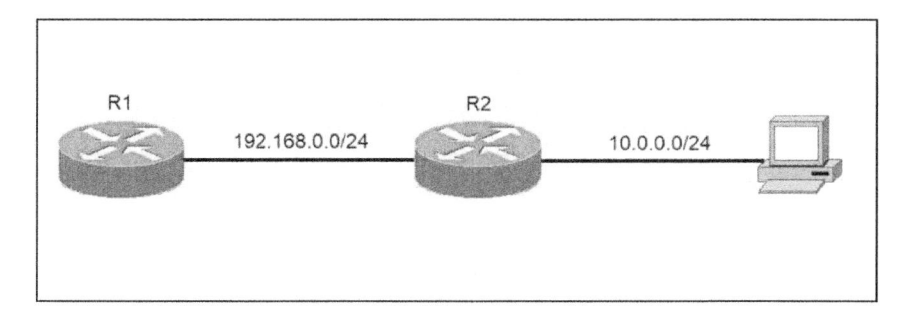

The RIP configuration on R2 looks like this:

```
router rip
 version 2
 network 10.0.0.0
 network 192.168.0.0
```

As we've already mentioned, the network command does two things:

- ❖ Advertises the defined network in RIP.
- ❖ Activates RIP on the interfaces whose addresses fall within the specified classful networks.

So, in the example network above, RIP will also be activated on the interface connected to the workstation on the right. This means that the workstation will also receive RIP updates, which is pointless. To prevent this from happening, the passive interface command is used:

```
R2(config)#router rip
R2(config-router)#passive-interface Gi0/1
```

Now, the RIP process will no longer send RIP updates out the Gi0/1 interface. However, all received RIP updates will be processed and the subnet 10.0.0.0/24 will still be advertised.

RIP loop prevention

Distance vector protocols are susceptible to routing loops. Routing loops occur when a packet is continually routed through the same routers over and over again, in an endless circle. Because they can render a network unusable, distance vector routing protocols (such as RIP and EIGRP) employ several different mechanisms to prevent routing loops. We will describe them in this article.

Split Horizon

Split horizon is one of the features of distance vector routing protocols that prevents routing loops. This feature prevents a router from advertising a route back onto the interface from which it was learned.

Consider the following network topology:

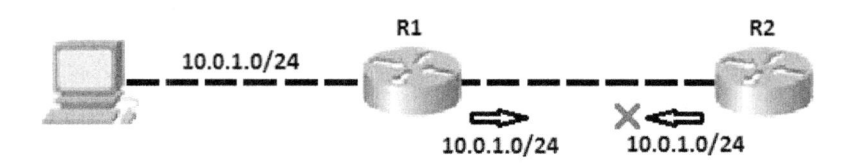

```
       R1                    R2
10.0.1.0/24 ━━━━━━━━━━━━━━━━━
            10.0.1.0/24  10.0.1.0/24
```

Router R1 has a route to the subnet 10.0.1.0/24 that is advertised to router R2 by using RIP. Router R2 receives the update and stores the route in its routing table. Router R2 knows that the routing update for that route has come from R1, so it won't advertise the route back to router R1. Otherwise, if the network 10.0.1.0/24 goes down, router R1 could receive a route to the subnet 10.0.1.0/24 from R2. Router R1 would think that R2 has the route to reach the subnet and would send packets destinated for the 10.0.1.0/24 to R2. R2 would receive the packets from R1 and sends them back to R1, because R2 thinks that R1 has a route to reach the subnet, thereby creating a routing loop.

Route poisoning

Route poisoning is another method for preventing routing loops employed by distance vector routing protocols. When a router detects that one of its directly connected routes has failed, it sends the advertisement for that route with an infinite metric (poisoning the route). A router that receives the update knows that the route has failed and doesn't use it anymore.

Consider the following example:

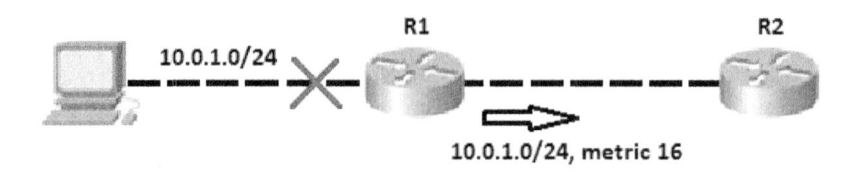

```
                 R1                    R2
10.0.1.0/24 ━━━━━━━━━━━━━━━━━━━━━
                 10.0.1.0/24, metric 16
```

Router R1 is directly connected to the 10.0.1.0/24 subnet. Router R1 runs RIP and the subnet is advertised to R2. When the R1's Fa0/1 interface fails, the route advertisement is sent by R1 to R2 indicating that the route has failed. The route has a metric of 16, which is more than the RIP's maximum hop count of 15, so R1 considers the route to be unreachable.

Hold down timer

Hold down is another loop-prevention mechanism employed by distance vector routing protocol. This feature prevents a router from learning new information about a failed route. When a router receives the information about the unreachable route, the Hold down timer is started. The router ignores all routing updates for that route until the timer expires (by default, 180 seconds in RIP). Only updates allowed during that period are updates sent from the router that originally advertised the route. If that router advertises the update, the Hold down timer is stopped, and the routing information is processed.

An example will help you understand the concept better. Consider the following network topology.

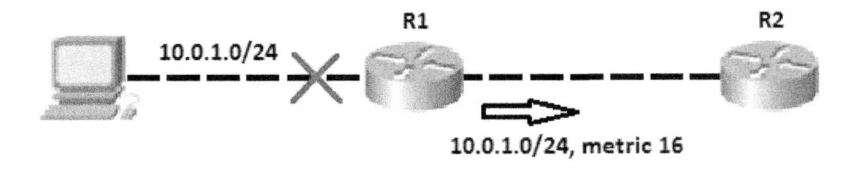

Router R1 has advertised its directly connected subnet 10.0.1.0/24 through RIP. After some period of time, the interface Fa0/1 on R1 fails and the router R1 sends the poisoned route to R2. R2 receives the routing update, marks the route as unreachable and starts the Hold down timer. During that time all updates from any other routers about that route are ignored to prevent routing loops. If interface Fa0/1 on R1 comes back up, R1 again advertises the route. R2 process that update even if the Hold down timer is still running, because the update is sent by the same router that originally advertised the route.

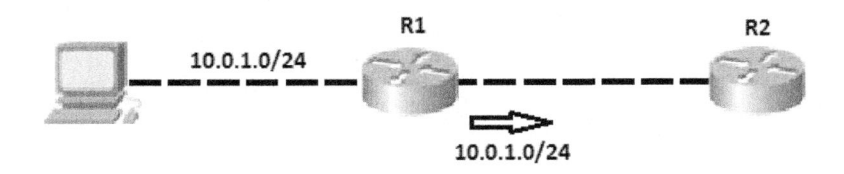

Advertise default routes using RIP

Consider the following example network:

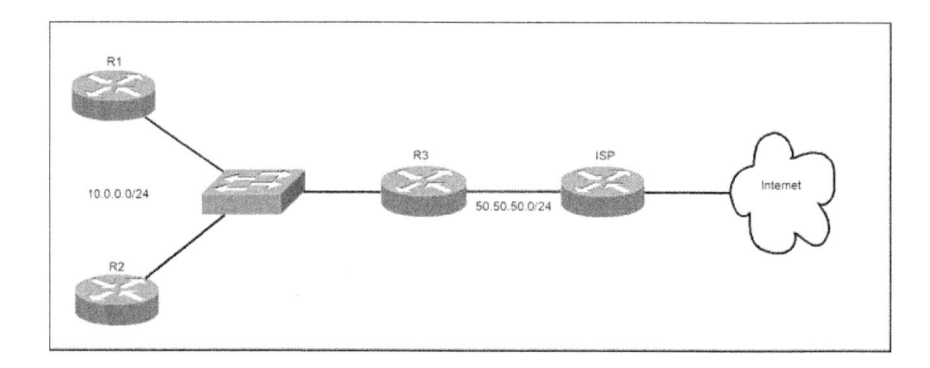

In the network above we have three routers running RIP. Router R3 is connected to the ISP's internet router and has a static default route that points to it. It is possible to advertise that default route using RIP to other routers in the local network. On R3, we simply need to enter the default-information originate command in the RIP configuration mode.

Here is the configuration on R3:

```
R3(config)#ip route 0.0.0.0 0.0.0.0 50.50.50.1
R3(config)#router rip
R3(config-router)#default-information originate
```

R1 and R2 don't need any additional configuration – they learn the default route just like any other RIP route:

```
R1#show ip route rip
R*   0.0.0.0/0 [120/1] via 10.0.0.1, 00:00:04, GigabitEthernet0/0
```

IPART IV: EIGRP

EIGRP overview

EIGRP (Enhanced Interior Gateway Routing Protocol) is an advanced distance vector routing protocol. This protocol is an evolution of an earlier Cisco protocol called IGRP, which is now considered obsolete. EIGRP supports classless routing and VLSM, route summarization, incremental updates, load balancing and many other useful features. It is a Cisco proprietary protocol, so all routers in a network that is running EIGRP must be Cisco routers.

Routers running EIGRP must become neighbors before exchanging routing information. To dynamically discover neighbors, EIGRP routers use the multicast address of 224.0.0.10. Each EIGRP router stores routing and topology information in three tables:

- Neighbor table – stores information about EIGRP neighbors
- Topology table – stores routing information learned from neighboring routers
- Routing table – stores the best routes

Administrative distance of EIGRP is 90, which is less than both the administrative distance of RIP and the administrative distance of OSPF, so EIGRP routes will be preferred over these routes. EIGRP uses Reliable Transport Protocol (RTP) for sending messages.

EIGRP calculates its metric by using bandwidth, delay, reliability, and load. By default, only bandwidth and delay are used when calculating metric, while reliability and load are set to zero.

EIGPR uses the concept of autonomous systems. An autonomous system is a set of EIGRP enabled routers that should become EIGRP neighbors. Each router inside an autonomous system must have the same autonomous system number configured, otherwise routers will not become neighbors.

EIGRP Neighbors

EIGRP must establish neighbor relationships with other EIGRP neighboring routers before exchanging routing information. To establish a neighbor relationships, routers send hello packets every couple of seconds. Hello packets are sent to the multicast address of 224.0.0.10.NOTE

On LAN interfaces hellos are sent every 5 seconds. On WAN interfaces every 60 seconds.

The following fields in a hello packet must be the identical in order for routers to become neighbors:

- ASN (autonomous system number)
- Subnet number
- K values (components of metric)

Routers send hello packets every couple of seconds to ensure that the neighbor relationship is still active. By default, routers consider the neighbor to be down after a hold-down timer has expired. Hold-down timer is, by default, three times the hello interval. On LAN network the hold-down timer is 15 seconds.

Feasible and reported distance

Two terms that you will often encounter when working with EIGRP are feasible and reported distance. Let's clarify these terms:

- Feasible distance (FD) – the metric of the best route to reach a network. That route will be listed in the routing table.
- Reported distance (RD) – the metric advertised by a neighboring router for a specific route. In other words, it is the metric of the route used by the neighboring router to reach the network.

To better understand the concept, consider the following example.

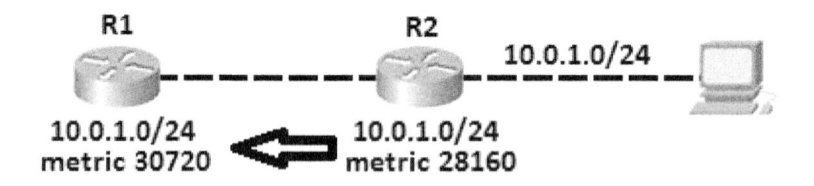

```
        R1                  R2
                                    10.0.1.0/24
     ---X---------------X------------[PC]

   10.0.1.0/24      10.0.1.0/24
   metric 30720  ⇐  metric 28160
```

EIGRP has been configured on R1 and R2. R2 is directly connected to the subnet 10.0.1.0/24 and advertises that subnet into EIGRP. Let's say that R2's metric to reach that subnet is 28160. When the subnet is advertised to R1, R2 informs R1 that its metric to reach 10.0.1.0/24 is 28160. From the R1's perspective that metric is considered to be the reported distance for that route. R1 receives the update and adds the metric to the neighbor to the reported distance. That metric is called the feasible distance and is stored in R1's routing table (30720 in our case).

The feasible and reported distance are displayed in R1's EIGRP topology table:

```
R1#show ip eigrp topology
IP-EIGRP Topology Table for AS 1/ID(192.168.0.1)
Codes: P - Passive, A - Active, U - Update, Q - Query, R - Reply,
       r - Reply status
```

52

P 10.0.1.0/24, 1 successors, FD is 30720
    via 192.168.0.2 (30720/28160), FastEthernet0/0
P 192.168.0.0/24, 1 successors, FD is 28160
    via Connected, FastEthernet0/0

Successor and feasible successor

Another two terms that appear often in the EIGRP world are successor and feasible successor. A successor is the route with the best metric to reach a destination. That route is stored in the routing table. A feasible successor is a backup path to reach that same destination that can be used immediately if the successor route fails. These backup routes are stored in the topology table.

For a route to be chosen as a feasible successor, one condition must be met:

- The neighbor's advertised distance (AD) for the route must be less than the successor's feasible distance (FD).

The following example explains the concept of a successor and a feasible successor.

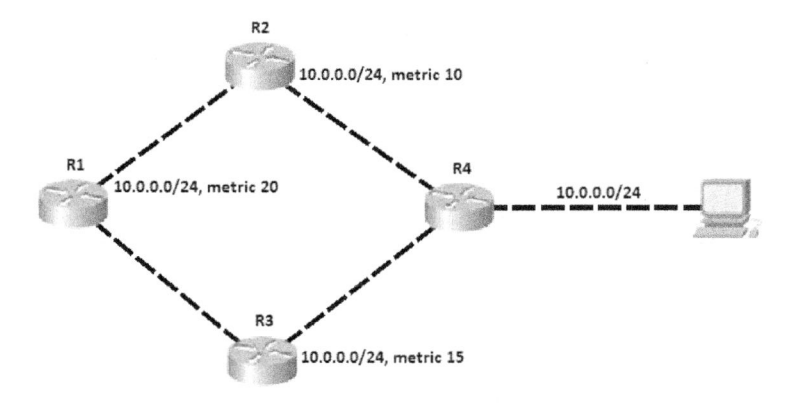

R1 has two paths to reach the subnet 10.0.0.0/24. The path through R2 has the best metric (20) and it is stored in the R1's routing table. The other route, through R3, is a feasible successor route, because the feasibility condition has been met (R3's advertised distance of 15 is less than R1's feasible distance of 20). R1 stores that route in the topology table. This route can be immediately used if the primary route fails.

EIGRP topology table

EIGRP topology table contains all learned routes to a destination. The table holds all routes received from a neighbor, successors and feasible successors for every route, and interfaces on which updates were received. The table also holds all locally connected subnets included in an EIGRP process.

Best routes (the successors) from the topology table are stored in the routing table. Feasible successors are only stored in the topology table and can be used immediately if the primary route fails.

Consider the following network topology.

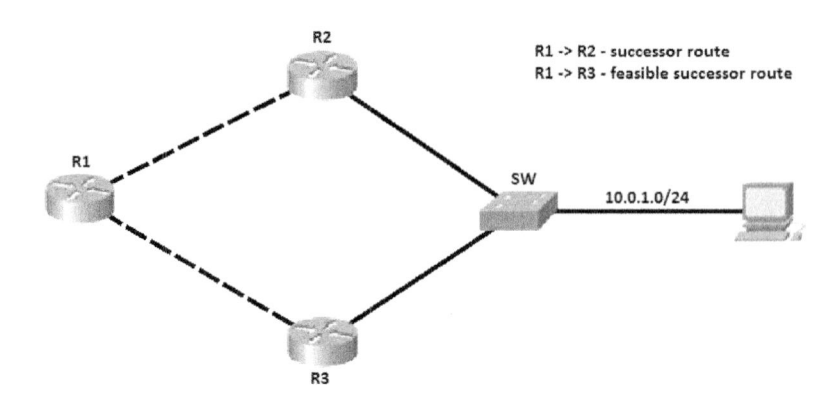

R1 -> R2 - successor route
R1 -> R3 - feasible successor route

EIGRP is running on all three routers. Routers R2 and R3 both connect to the subnet 10.0.1.0/24 and advertise that subnet to R1. R1 receives both updates and calculates the best route. The best path goes through R2, so R1 stores that route in the routing table. Router R1 also calculates the metric of the route through R3. Let's say that advertised distance of that route is less then feasible distance of the best route. The feasibility condition is met and router R1 stores that route in the topology table as a feasible successor route. The route can be used immediately if the primary route fails.

EIGRP configuration

Configuring EIGRP 1

EIGRP configuration closely resembles RIP configuration. Only two steps are required:

- ❖ Enabling EIGRP by using the router eigrp ASN_NUMBER command
- ❖ Telling EIGRP which networks to advertise by using one or more network statements

The first command, router eigrp ASN_NUMBER, enables EIGRP on a router. ASN_NUMBER represents an autonomous system number and must be the same on all routers running EIGRP, otherwise routers won't become neighbors. The second command, network SUBNET, enables EIGRP on selected interfaces and specifies which networks will be advertised. By default, the network command takes a classful network number as the parameter.

To illustrate a configuration of EIGRP, we will use the following network:

```
                    R1              R2
    10.0.0.0/24          172.16.0.0/16        192.168.0.0/24
```

The network depicted above consists of only two routers. Each router has a directly connected subnet that needs to be advertised through EIGRP. Here is the EIGRP configuration on R1 and R2:

```
R1(config)#router eigrp 1
R1(config-router)#network 10.0.0.0
R1(config-router)#network 172.16.0.0
R1(config-router)#
```

```
R2(config)#router eigrp 1
R2(config-router)#network 192.168.0.0
R2(config-router)#network 172.16.0.0
R2(config-router)#
```

You can verify that routers have become neighbors by using the show ip eigrp neighbors command on either router:

```
R1#show ip eigrp neighbors
IP-EIGRP neighbors for process 1
H   Address         Interface     Hold Uptime   SRTT  RTO   Q    Seq
                                  (sec)         (ms)        Cnt  Num
0   172.16.0.2      Fa0/0         12   00:01:25 40    1000  0    3
```

The command above lists all EIGRP neighbors. The address field lists the neighboring router RID (router ID). The interface field shows on which local interface the neighbor relationship has been formed.

You can verify that routes are indeed being exchanged by using the show ip route command on both routers:

R1:

55

```
R1#show ip route
Codes: C - connected, S - static, I - IGRP, R - RIP, M - mobile, B - BGP
       D - EIGRP, EX - EIGRP external, O - OSPF, IA - OSPF inter area
       N1 - OSPF NSSA external type 1, N2 - OSPF NSSA external type 2
       E1 - OSPF external type 1, E2 - OSPF external type 2, E - EGP
       i - IS-IS, L1 - IS-IS level-1, L2 - IS-IS level-2, ia - IS-IS inter area
       * - candidate default, U - per-user static route, o - ODR
       P - periodic downloaded static route

Gateway of last resort is not set

     10.0.0.0/24 is subnetted, 1 subnets
C       10.0.0.0 is directly connected, FastEthernet0/1
C    172.16.0.0/16 is directly connected, FastEthernet0/0
D    192.168.0.0/24 [90/30720] via 172.16.0.2, 00:00:03, FastEthernet0/0
R1#
```

R2:

```
R2#show ip route
Codes: C - connected, S - static, I - IGRP, R - RIP, M - mobile, B - BGP
       D - EIGRP, EX - EIGRP external, O - OSPF, IA - OSPF inter area
       N1 - OSPF NSSA external type 1, N2 - OSPF NSSA external type 2
       E1 - OSPF external type 1, E2 - OSPF external type 2, E - EGP
       i - IS-IS, L1 - IS-IS level-1, L2 - IS-IS level-2, ia - IS-IS inter area
       * - candidate default, U - per-user static route, o - ODR
       P - periodic downloaded static route

Gateway of last resort is not set

     10.0.0.0/24 is subnetted, 1 subnets
D       10.0.0.0 [90/30720] via 172.16.0.1, 00:00:02, FastEthernet0/0
C    172.16.0.0/16 is directly connected, FastEthernet0/0
C    192.168.0.0/24 is directly connected, FastEthernet0/1
R2#
```

NOTE

The D character at the beginning of a line in a routing table indicates that the route has been learned via EIGRP.

Configuring EIGRP 2

By default, the network command uses a classful network as the parameter. All interfaces inside that classful network will participate in the EIGRP process. To enable EIGRP only on specific interfaces, a wildcard mask can be used. The syntax of the command is:

(router-eigrp) network WILDCARD_MASK

Consider the following example.

```
                    R1
     10.0.0.0/24   ┌──┐   10.0.1.0/24
  ═══════════════  │  │  ═══════════════
                   └──┘
                   Fa0/0
```

Router R1 has two directly connected subnets, 10.0.0.0/24 and 10.0.1.0/24. We want to enable EIGRP only on the subnet connected to the interface Fa0/0. If we enter the network 10.0.0.0 command under the EIGRP configuration mode, both subnets will be included in EIGRP process because we've used a classful network number in the network command. To configure EIGRP only on interface Fa0/0, the network 10.0.0.0 0.0.0.255 command can be used. This will enable EIGRP only on interfaces starting with 10.0.0.X.

```
R1(config)#router eigrp 1
R1(config-router)#network 10.0.0.0 0.0.0.255
R1(config-router)#
```

By using the command show ip protocols, you can verify that only the network 10.0.0.0/24 is included in EIGRP:

```
R1#show ip protocols
Routing Protocol is "eigrp 1 "
  Outgoing update filter list for all interfaces is not set
  Incoming update filter list for all interfaces is not set
  Default networks flagged in outgoing updates
  Default networks accepted from incoming updates
  EIGRP metric weight K1=1, K2=0, K3=1, K4=0, K5=0
  EIGRP maximum hopcount 100
  EIGRP maximum metric variance 1
Redistributing: eigrp 1
  Automatic network summarization is in effect
  Automatic address summarization:
  Maximum path: 4
  Routing for Networks:
    10.0.0.0/24
  Routing Information Sources:
    Gateway         Distance      Last Update
  Distance: internal 90 external 170

R1#
```

Wildcard mask in EIGRP

The network command in EIGRP uses a classful network as the parameter by default, which means that all interfaces inside the classful network will participate in the EIGRP process. We can enable EIGRP only for specific networks using **wildcard masks**. The syntax of the command is:

```
(router-eigrp)#network IP_ADDRESS WILDCARD_MASK
```

We will use the following example network:

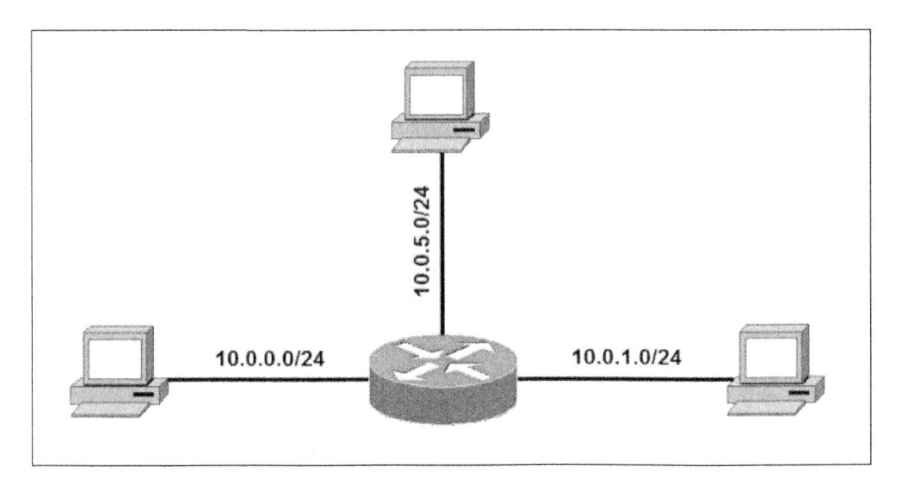

[Network diagram: A router directly connected to three subnets — 10.0.0.0/24, 10.0.1.0/24, and 10.0.5.0/24]

The router is directly connected to three subnets. Let's say that we want to advertise only the 10.0.0.0/24 subnet in EIGRP. We can use the wildcard mask of 0.0.0.255 to do this:

```
R1(config-router)#network 10.0.0.0 0.0.0.255
Using the show ip protocols command we can verify that only the subnet
10.0.0.0/24 is included in EIGRP:R1#show ip protocols
Routing Protocol is "eigrp 1 "
Outgoing update filter list for all interfaces is not set
Incoming update filter list for all interfaces is not set
Default networks flagged in outgoing updates
Default networks accepted from incoming updates
EIGRP metric weight K1=1, K2=0, K3=1, K4=0, K5=0
EIGRP maximum hopcount 100
EIGRP maximum metric variance 1
Redistributing: eigrp 1
Automatic network summarization is in effect
Automatic address summarization:
Maximum path: 4
Routing for Networks:
10.0.0.0/24
```

58

> Routing Information Sources:
> Gateway Distance Last Update
> Distance: internal 90 external 170

Notice that 10.0.0.0/24 is listed under the Routing for Networks column. The other two networks (10.0.1.0/24 and 10.0.5.0/24) are not included in EIGRP.

EIGRP automatic & manual summarization

Route summarization is a method of representing multiple networks with a single summary address. It is often use in large networks with many subnets because it reduces the number of routes that a router must maintain and minimizes the traffic used for routing updates. Two methods for summarizing routes exist: automatic summarization and manual summarization.

EIGRP automatic summarization

By default, EIGRP has the auto summary feature enabled. Because of this, routes are summarized to classful address at network boundaries in the routing updates.

To better understand the concept of auto-summarization, consider the following example.

Router R1 and R2 are running EIGRP. Router R1 has the locally connected subnet 10.0.1.0/24 that is advertised to the router R2. Because of the auto summary feature, the router R1 summarizes the network 10.0.1.0/24 before sending the route to R2. With the auto summary feature turned on, R1 sends the classful route 10.0.0.0/8 to R2 instead of the more specific 10.0.1.0/24 route.

On R1, we have configured the following network statement:

```
R1(config)#router eigrp 1
R1(config-router)#network 10.0.1.0
R1(config-router)#
```

But, because of the auto-summary feature, R2 receives the route to the classful network 10.0.0.0/8:

```
R2#show ip route
Codes: C - connected, S - static, I - IGRP, R - RIP, M - mobile, B - BGP
       D - EIGRP, EX - EIGRP external, O - OSPF, IA - OSPF inter area
       N1 - OSPF NSSA external type 1, N2 - OSPF NSSA external type 2
       E1 - OSPF external type 1, E2 - OSPF external type 2, E - EGP
       i - IS-IS, L1 - IS-IS level-1, L2 - IS-IS level-2, ia - IS-IS inter area
       * - candidate default, U - per-user static route, o - ODR
       P - periodic downloaded static route

Gateway of last resort is not set

D    10.0.0.0/8 [90/30720] via 192.168.0.1, 00:06:56, FastEthernet0/0
C    192.168.0.0/24 is directly connected, FastEthernet0/0
R2#
```

The auto summary feature can cause problems with discontiguous networks. This is why this feature is usually turned off. This is done by using the no auto-summary command:

```
R1(config)#router eigrp 1
R1(config-router)#network 10.0.1.0
R1(config-router)#no auto-summary
R1(config-router)#
%DUAL-5-NBRCHANGE: IP-EIGRP 1: Neighbor 192.168.0.2 (FastEthernet0/0) is up: new
 adjacency

R1(config-router)#
```

Now R2 has the classless route to reach the subnet 10.0.1.0/24:

```
R2#show ip route
Codes: C - connected, S - static, I - IGRP, R - RIP, M - mobile, B - BGP
       D - EIGRP, EX - EIGRP external, O - OSPF, IA - OSPF inter area
       N1 - OSPF NSSA external type 1, N2 - OSPF NSSA external type 2
       E1 - OSPF external type 1, E2 - OSPF external type 2, E - EGP
       i - IS-IS, L1 - IS-IS level-1, L2 - IS-IS level-2, ia - IS-IS inter area
       * - candidate default, U - per-user static route, o - ODR
       P - periodic downloaded static route

Gateway of last resort is not set

     10.0.0.0/24 is subnetted, 1 subnets
D       10.0.1.0 [90/30720] via 192.168.0.1, 00:02:47, FastEthernet0/0
C    192.168.0.0/24 is directly connected, FastEthernet0/0
R2#
```

> NOTE
>
> After typing the no auto-summary command, the neighbor relationship will be re-established.

EIGRP manual summarization

One of the advantages of EIGRP over some other routing protocols (like OSPF) is that manual summarization can be done on any router within a network. A single route can be used to represent multiple routes, which reduces the size of routing tables in a network.

Manual summarization is configured on a per-interface basis. The syntax of the command is:

> (config-if) ip summary-address eigrp ASN SUMMARY_ADDRESS SUBNET_MASK

An example will help you to understand the concept of manual summarization:

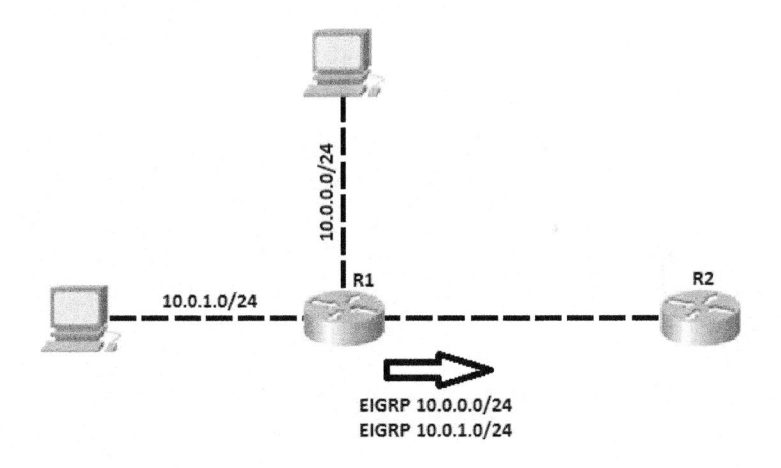

```
                          10.0.0.0/24
                              |
                              |
         10.0.1.0/24           R1                    R2
        -------------------- [R1] ------------------ [R2]

                         EIGRP 10.0.0.0/24
                         EIGRP 10.0.1.0/24
```

Router R1 and R2 are running EIGRP. Router R1 (on the left) has two directly connected subnets: 10.0.0.0/24 and 10.0.1.0/24. EIGRP advertises these subnets as two separate routes. R2 now has two routes for two subnets, which can be confirmed by using the show ip route command on R2:

61

```
R2#show ip route
Codes: C - connected, S - static, I - IGRP, R - RIP, M - mobile, B - BGP
       D - EIGRP, EX - EIGRP external, O - OSPF, IA - OSPF inter area
       N1 - OSPF NSSA external type 1, N2 - OSPF NSSA external type 2
       E1 - OSPF external type 1, E2 - OSPF external type 2, E - EGP
       i - IS-IS, L1 - IS-IS level-1, L2 - IS-IS level-2, ia - IS-IS inter area
       * - candidate default, U - per-user static route, o - ODR
       P - periodic downloaded static route

Gateway of last resort is not set

     10.0.0.0/24 is subnetted, 2 subnets
D       10.0.0.0 [90/284160] via 192.168.0.1, 00:00:15, FastEthernet0/0
D       10.0.1.0 [90/30720] via 192.168.0.1, 00:00:28, FastEthernet0/0
C    192.168.0.0/24 is directly connected, FastEthernet0/0
R2#
```

We could configure R1 to advertise only one summary route for both subnets, which helps reduce R2's routing table. To do this, the following command can be used:

```
R1(config)#int fa0/0
R1(config-if)#ip summary-address eigrp 1 10.0.0.0 255.255.0.0
R1(config-if)#
%DUAL-5-NBRCHANGE: IP-EIGRP 1: Neighbor 192.168.0.2 (FastEthernet0/0) is up: new
 adjacency
```

Now, R1 is sending only one route to reach both subnets to R2. We can verify that by using the show ip route command on R2

```
R2#show ip route
Codes: C - connected, S - static, I - IGRP, R - RIP, M - mobile, B - BGP
       D - EIGRP, EX - EIGRP external, O - OSPF, IA - OSPF inter area
       N1 - OSPF NSSA external type 1, N2 - OSPF NSSA external type 2
       E1 - OSPF external type 1, E2 - OSPF external type 2, E - EGP
       i - IS-IS, L1 - IS-IS level-1, L2 - IS-IS level-2, ia - IS-IS inter area
       * - candidate default, U - per-user static route, o - ODR
       P - periodic downloaded static route

Gateway of last resort is not set

     10.0.0.0/16 is subnetted, 1 subnets
D       10.0.0.0 [90/30720] via 192.168.0.1, 00:00:06, FastEthernet0/0
C    192.168.0.0/24 is directly connected, FastEthernet0/0
```

Now R2 has only one route to reach both subnets on R1.

> **NOTE**
>
> In the example above, the ip summary command included two subnets on R1, but also some other addresses that are not in these subnets. The range of the summarized addresses is 10.0.0.0 – 10.0.255.255, so R2 thinks that R1 has the routes for all addresses inside that range. That could cause some problems if these addresses exist somewhere else in the network.

EIGRP authentication & load balancing

EIGRP authentication

EIGRP authentication is used to prevent an attacker from forming the EIGRP neighbor relationship with your router and advertising incorrect routing information. By using the same pre-shared key (PSK) on all routers you can force EIGRP to authenticate each EIGRP message. That way you can ensure that your router accepts routing updates only from the trusted sources. To authenticate every message, the MD5 (Message Digest 5) algorithm is used.

Three steps are required to configure EIGRP authentication:

1. Creating a keychain
2. Specifying a key string for a key
3. Configuring EIGRP to use authentication

EIGRP uses the concept of key chains. Each key chain can have many keys, just like in real life. You can specify a different lifetime interval of each key. That way the second key in a key chain can be used after the first one is expired, the third one after the second and so on. After you have created a key chain with the corresponding keys, you need to enable EIGRP authentication for a particular interface.

To configure a router to use EIGRP configuration the following commands are used:

(config-if) ip authentication key-chain eigrp ASN KEY_CHAIN_NAME – specifies the name of the key chain that will be used for authentication

> **NOTE**
>
> For the authentication to work, the key number and the key string have to match on both routers! The key chain name doesn't have to be the same on both routers.

The following example shows how EIGRP authentication is configured:

```
R1(config)#key chain study-ccna.com
R1(config-keychain)#key 1
R1(config-keychain-key)#key-string very_secret
R1(config-keychain-key)#interface fa0/0
R1(config-if)#ip authentication mode eigrp 1 md5
R1(config-if)#ip authentication key-chain eigrp 1 study-ccna.com
```

To establish a time frame for the validity of a key, you need to configure the accept-lifetime and the send-lifetime parameters. The syntax of the commands is:

> (config-keychain-key) accept-lifetime start_time {infinite | end_time | duration seconds}
> (config-keychain-key) send-lifetime start_time {infinite | end_time | duration seconds}

The first command specifies the time period during which the key will be accepted. The second command specifies the time period during which the key will be sent.

For example, if we want to use a key only from January 1st, 2013 to December 1st, 2013, the following commands are used:

```
R1(config-keychain-key)#accept-lifetime 00:00:00 Jan 1 2013 00:00:00 Dec 1 2013
R1(config-keychain-key)#send-lifetime 00:00:00 Jan 1 2013 00:00:00 Dec 1 2013
```

EIGRP load balancing

By default, EIGRP supports equal-cost load balancing over four links. Equal cost means that multiple routes must have the same metric to reach the destination, so that router can choose to load balance across equal cost links.

To better understand the equal-cost load balancing concept, consider the following example.

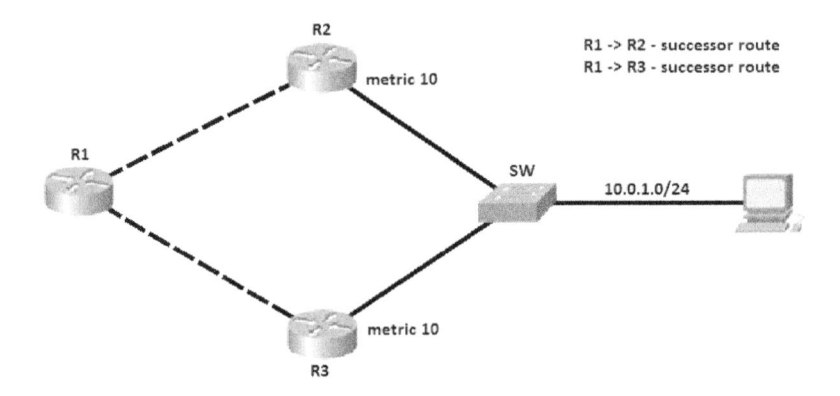

All three routers are running EIGRP. Routers R2 and R3 are connected to the subnet 10.0.1.0/24. Both routers advertise the route to reach that subnet to R1. Router R1 receives the two routing updates for the subnet 10.0.1.0/24 with the same metric (the metric is the same because both routers connect to the subnet 10.0.1.0/24 and R1 across the links with the same bandwidth and delay values). Router R1 places both routes in the routing table and load balances across three links.

You can verify that R1 is indeed using both paths by typing the show ip route command:

```
R1#show ip route
Codes: C - connected, S - static, I - IGRP, R - RIP, M - mobile, B - BGP
       D - EIGRP, EX - EIGRP external, O - OSPF, IA - OSPF inter area
       N1 - OSPF NSSA external type 1, N2 - OSPF NSSA external type 2
       E1 - OSPF external type 1, E2 - OSPF external type 2, E - EGP
       i - IS-IS, L1 - IS-IS level-1, L2 - IS-IS level-2, ia - IS-IS inter area
       * - candidate default, U - per-user static route, o - ODR
       P - periodic downloaded static route

Gateway of last resort is not set

     10.0.0.0/24 is subnetted, 1 subnets
D       10.0.1.0 [90/284160] via 192.168.0.2, 00:05:28, FastEthernet0/0
                 [90/284160] via 172.16.0.2, 00:05:28, FastEthernet0/1
C    172.16.0.0/16 is directly connected, FastEthernet0/1
C    192.168.0.0/24 is directly connected, FastEthernet0/0
```

One of the advantages of EIGRP is that, unlike OSPF and many other routing protocols, EIGRP also supports unequal-cost load balancing. You can set up your router to load balance over links with different metric to reach the destination. To accomplish unequal-cost load balancing, the variance command is used. The command takes one parameter, the multiplier, which tells the router to load balance across each link with the metric for the destination less than the feasible distance multiplied by the multiplier value.

> NOTE
>
> The multiplier value, by default, is 1. The maximum value is 128.

Consider the following example.

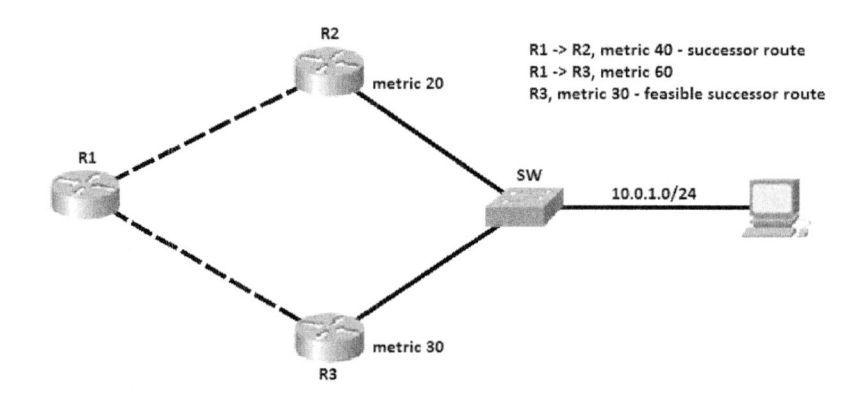

R1 -> R2, metric 40 - successor route
R1 -> R3, metric 60
R3, metric 30 - feasible successor route

All three routers are running EIGRP. Routers R2 and R3 are connected to the subnet 10.0.1.0/24. Both routers advertise the route to reach that subnet to R1. Router R1 chooses the route from R2 as the best route. Let's say that R1 calculated the metric of 40 for the path through R2. That route is placed in the R1's routing table. But what if we want to load balance traffic across the other link? The route through R3 has a feasible distance of 30, which is less than the metric of the successor route, so the feasibility condition has been met and that route has been placed in the R1's topology table. Let's say that R1 calculated the metric of 60 for the route through R3. To enable load balancing across that link, you need to use the variance command:

(router-eigrp) variance MULTIPLIER

In our example, the variance 2 command can be used. This tells the router to load balance across any links with the metric less than 80 (because 40 times 2 is 80). The route through R3 is added to the routing table.

NOTE

A path must be a feasible successor route to be used in unequal load balancing.

EIGRP Reliable Transport Protocol (RTP)

EIGRP doesn't send messages with UDP or TCP; instead, a Cisco's protocol called Reliable Transport Protocol (RTP) is used for communication between EIGRP-speaking routers. As the name implies, reliability is a key feature of this protocol, and it is designed to enable quick delivery of updates and tracking of data reception.

Five different packets types are used by EIGRP:

* Update – contains route information. When routing updates are sent in response to the metric or topology changes, reliable multicasts are used.

In the event that only one router needs an update, for example when a new neighbor is discovered, unicasts are used.
- ❖ Query – a request for specific routes that always uses the reliable multicast method. Routers send queries when they realize they've lost the path to a particular network and are looking for alternative paths.
- ❖ Reply – sent in response to a query via the unicast method. Replies can include a specific route to the queried destination or declare that there is no known route.
- ❖ Hello – used to discover EIGRP neighbors. It is sent via unreliable multicast and no acknowledgment is required.
- ❖ Acknowledgment (ACK) – sent in response to an update and is always unicast. ACKs are not sent reliably.

> NOTE
>
> The acronym RTP is also used for a different protocol – Real-time Transport Protocol (RTP), used for VoIP communication.

EIGRP Diffusing Update Algorithm (DUAL)

Diffusing Update Algorithm (DUAL) is an algorithm used by EIGRP to select and maintain the best route to each remote network. DUAL is also used for the following purposes:

- ❖ Discover a backup route if there is one available.
- ❖ Support for variable length subnet masks (VLSMs).
- ❖ Perform dynamic route recoveries.
- ❖ Query neighbors for unknown alternate routes.
- ❖ Send out queries for alternate routes.

EIGRP stores all routes advertised by all EIGRP neighbors. The metric of these routes is used by DUAL to select the efficient and loop free paths. DUAL selects routes that will be inserted into the routing table. If a route fails, and there is no feasible successor, DUAL chooses a replacement route, which usually takes a couple of seconds.

The following requirements must be met in order for DUAL to work properly:

- ❖ EIGRP neighbors must discovered.
- ❖ All transmitted EIGRP messages should be received correctly.

all changes and messages should be processed in the order in which they're detected.

EIGRP summary

Here is a list of the most important EIGRP features:

- ❖ Advanced distance vector routing protocol

67

- ❖ Classless routing protocol
- ❖ Supports VLSM (Variable Length Subnet Mask)
- ❖ Converges fast
- ❖ Supports multiple Network layer protocols (IPv4, IPv6, IPX, AppleTalk…)
- ❖ Uses multicast address of 224.0.0.10 for routing updates
- ❖ Sends partial routing updates
- ❖ Supports equal and unequal-cost load balancing
- ❖ Supports manual summarization on any router within a network
- ❖ By default, uses bandwidth and delay to calculate its metric
- ❖ Cisco proprietary
- ❖ Supports MD5 authentication

PART V: OSPF

OSPF overview

OSPF (Open Shortest Path First) is a link state routing protocol. Because it is an open standard, it is implemented by a variety of network vendors. OSPF will run on most routers that doesn't necessarily have to be Cisco routers (unlike EIGRP which can be run only on Cisco routers).

Here are the most important features of OSPF:

- a classless routing protocol
- supports VLSM, CIDR, manual route summarization, equal cost load balancing
- incremental updates are supported
- uses only one parameter as the metric – the interface cost.
- the administrative distance of OSPF routes is, by default, 110.
- uses multicast addresses 224.0.0.5 and 224.0.0.6 for routing updates.

Routers running OSPF must establish neighbor relationships before exchanging routes. Because OSPF is a link state routing protocol, neighbors don't exchange routing tables. Instead, they exchange information about network topology. Each OSFP router then runs SFP algorithm to calculate the best routes and adds those to the routing table. Because each router knows the entire topology of a network, the chance for a routing loop to occur is minimal.

Each OSPF router stores routing and topology information in three tables:

- **Neighbor table** – stores information about OSPF neighbors
- **Topology table** – stores the topology structure of a network
- **Routing table** – stores the best routes

OSPF neighbors

OSPF routers need to establish a neighbor relationship before exchanging routing updates. OSPF neighbors are dynamically discovered by sending Hello packets out each OSPF-enabled interface on a router. Hello packets are sent to the multicast IP address of 224.0.0.5.

The process is explained in the following figure:

```
              R1                           R2



           OSPF Hello            OSPF Hello
```

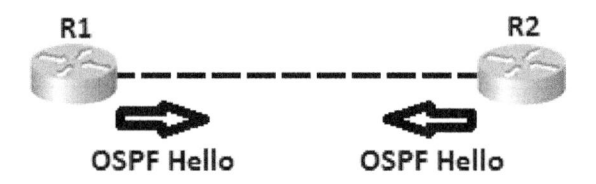

Routers R1 and R2 are directly connected. After OSFP is enabled both routers send Hellos to each other to establish a neighbor relationship. You can verify that the neighbor relationship has indeed been established by typing the show ip ospf neighbors command.

```
R1#show ip ospf neig

Neighbor ID      Pri    State           Dead Time    Address       Interface
2.2.2.2            1    FULL/DR         00:00:30     192.168.0.2   FastEthernet0/0
```

In the example above, you can see that the router-id of R2 is 2.2.2.2. Each OSPF router is assigned a router ID. A router ID is determined by using one of the following:

The following fields in the Hello packets must be the same on both routers in order for routers to become neighbors:

By default, OSPF sends hello packets every 10 second on an Ethernet network (Hello interval). A dead timer is four times the value of the hello interval, so if a router on an Ethernet network doesn't receive at least one Hello packet from an OSFP neighbor for 40 seconds, the routers declares that neighbor to be down.

OSPF neighbor states

Before establishing a neighbor relationship, OSPF routers need to go through several state changes. These states are explained below.

OSPF areas

OSPF uses the concept of areas. An area is a logical grouping of contiguous networks and routers. All routers in the same area have the same topology table, but they don't know about routers in the other areas. The main benefits of creating areas is that the size of the topology and the routing table on a router is reduced, less time is required to run the SFP algorithm and routing updates are also reduced.

Each area in the OSPF network must connect to the backbone area (area 0). All router inside an area must have the same area ID to become OSPF neighbors. A router that has interfaces in more than one area (area 0 and area 1, for example) is called Area Border Router (ABR). A router that connects an OSPF network to other routing domains (EIGRP network, for example) is called Autonomous System Border Router (ASBR).

> NOTE
>
> In OSPF, manual route summarization is possible only on ABRs and ASBRs.

To better understand the concept of areas, consider the following example.

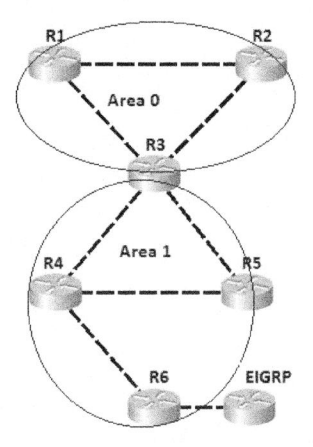

All routers are running OSPF. Routers R1 and R2 are inside the backbone area (area 0). Router R3 is an ABR, because it has interfaces in two areas, namely area 0 and area 1. Router R4 and R5 are inside area 1. Router R6 is an ASBR, because it connects OSFP network to another routing domain (an EIGRP domain in this case). If the R1's directly connected subnet fails, router R1 sends the routing update only to R2 and R3, because all routing updates all localized inside the area.

> NOTE
>
> The role of an ABR is to advertise address summaries to neighboring areas. The role of an ASBR is to connect an OSPF routing domain to another external network (e.g. Internet, EIGRP network…).

LSA, LSU and LSR

The LSAs (Link-State Advertisements) are used by OSPF routers to exchange topology information. Each LSA contains routing and topology information to describe a part of an OSPF network. When two neighbors decide to exchange routes, they send each other a list of all LSA in their respective topology database. Each router then checks its topology database and sends a Link State Request (LSR) message requesting all LSAs not found in its topology table. Other router responds with the Link State Update (LSU) that contains all LSAs requested by the other neighbor.

The concept is explained in the following example:

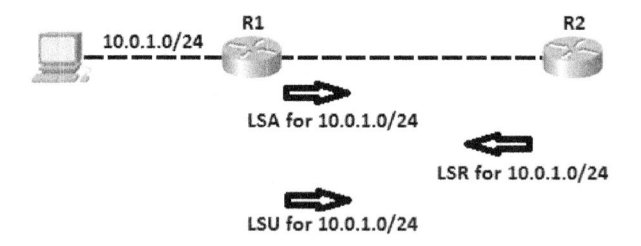

```
              R1                              R2
  10.0.1.0/24
              ─────────────────────────────────
              ▶ LSA for 10.0.1.0/24
                                   ◀ LSR for 10.0.1.0/24
              ▶ LSU for 10.0.1.0/24
```

After configuring OSPF on both routers, routers exchange LSAs to describe their respective topology database. Router R1 sends an LSA header for its directly connected network 10.0.1.0/24. Router R2 check its topology database and determines that it doesn't have information about that network. Router R2 then sends Link State Request message requesting further information about that network. Router R1 responds with Link State Update which contains information about subnet 10.0.1.0/24 (next hop address, cost…).

OSPF configuration

Configuring OSPF 1

OSPF basic configuration is very simple. Just like with other routing protocols covered so far (RIP, EIGRP) first you need to enable OSPF on a router. This is done by using the router ospf PROCESS-ID global configuration command. Next, you need to define on which interfaces OSPF will run and what networks will be advertised. This is done by using the network IP_ADDRESS WILDCARD_MASK AREA_ID command from the ospf configuration mode.

> **NOTE**
>
> The OSPF process number doesn't have to be the same on all routers in order to establish a neighbor relationship, but the Area ID has to be the same on all neighboring routers in order for routers to become neighbors.

Let's get started with some basic OSPF configuration. We will use the following network topology:

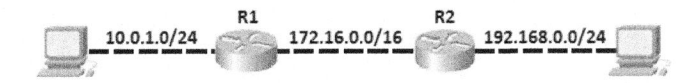

```
            R1              R2
  10.0.1.0/24   172.16.0.0/16   192.168.0.0/24
```

First, we need to enable OSPF on both routers. Then we need to define what network will be advertised into OSPF. This can be done by using the following sequence of commands on both routers:

```
R1(config-router)#router ospf 1
R1(config-router)#network 10.0.1.0 0.0.0.255 area 0
R1(config-router)#network 172.16.0.0 0.0.255.255 area 0
```

```
R2(config)#router ospf 1
R2(config-router)#network 192.168.0.0 0.0.0.255 area 0
R2(config-router)#network 172.16.0.0 0.0.255.255 area 0
```

The network commands entered on both routers include subnets directly connected to both routers. We can verify that the routers have become neighbors by typing the show ip ospf neighbors command on either router:

```
R1#show ip ospf neighbor

Neighbor ID     Pri   State         Dead Time   Address       Interface
192.168.0.2       1   FULL/BDR      00:00:32    172.16.0.2    FastEthernet0/1
```

To verify if the routing updated were exchanged, we can use the show ip route command. All routes marked with the character O are OSPF routes. For example, here is the output of the command on R1:

```
R1#show ip route
Codes: C - connected, S - static, I - IGRP, R - RIP, M - mobile, B - BGP
       D - EIGRP, EX - EIGRP external, O - OSPF, IA - OSPF inter area
       N1 - OSPF NSSA external type 1, N2 - OSPF NSSA external type 2
       E1 - OSPF external type 1, E2 - OSPF external type 2, E - EGP
       i - IS-IS, L1 - IS-IS level-1, L2 - IS-IS level-2, ia - IS-IS inter area
       * - candidate default, U - per-user static route, o - ODR
       P - periodic downloaded static route

Gateway of last resort is not set

     10.0.0.0/24 is subnetted, 1 subnets
C       10.0.1.0 is directly connected, FastEthernet0/0
C    172.16.0.0/16 is directly connected, FastEthernet0/1
O    192.168.0.0/24 [110/2] via 172.16.0.2, 00:03:44, FastEthernet0/1
```

You can see that R1 has learned about the network 192.168.0.0/24 through OSPF.

Configuring OSPF 2

Although basic OSPF configuration can be very simple, OSPF provides many extra features that can get really complex. In this example, we will configure multiarea OSPF network and some other OSPF features.

Consider the following multiarea OSPF network:

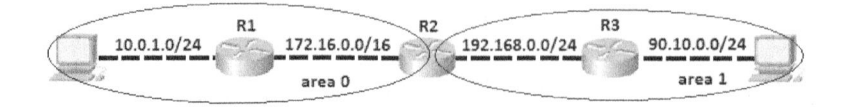

In this example we have two OSPF areas – area 0 and area 1. As you can see from the network topology depicted above, routers R1 and R3 are in the area 0 and area 1, respectively. Router 2 connects to both areas, which makes him an ABR (Area Border Router). Our goal is to advertise the subnets directly connected to R1 and R3. To do that, the following configuration on R1 will be used:

```
R1(config)#router ospf 1
R1(config-router)#network 10.0.1.0 0.0.0.255 area 0
R1(config-router)#network 172.16.0.0 0.0.255.255 area 0
R1(config-router)#router-id 1.1.1.1
```

> NOTE
>
> We have used the router-id 1.1.1.1 command to manually specify the router ID of this router. OSPF process will use that RID (router-id) when communicating with other OSPF neighbors.

Because R1 connects only to R2, we only need to establish a neighbor relationship with R2 and advertise directly connected subnet into OSPF.

Configuration of R3 looks similar, but with one difference, namely area number. R3 is in the area 1.

```
R3(config)#router ospf 1
R3(config-router)#network 192.168.0.0 0.0.0.255 area 1
R3(config-router)#network 90.10.0.0 0.0.0.255 area 1
R3(config-router)#router-id 3.3.3.3
```

What about R2? Well, because R2 is an ABR, we need to establish neighbor relationship with both R1 and R3. To do that, we need to specify different area ID for each neighbor relationship, 0 for R1 and 1 for R2. We can do that using the following sequence of commands:

```
R2(config)#router ospf 1
R2(config-router)#network 172.16.0.0 0.0.255.255 area 0
R2(config-router)#network 192.168.0.0 0.0.0.255 area 1
R2(config-router)#router-id 2.2.2.2
```

Now R2 should have neighbor relationship with both R1 and R3. We can verify that by using the show ip ospf neighbor command:

```
R2#show ip ospf neighbor

Neighbor ID     Pri   State          Dead Time   Address         Interface
1.1.1.1           1   FULL/BDR       00:00:39    172.16.0.1      FastEthernet0/0
3.3.3.3           1   FULL/DR        00:00:36    192.168.0.2     FastEthernet0/1
```

To verify if directly connected subnets are really advertised into the different area, we can use the show ip route ospf command on both R1 and R3:

```
R1#show ip route ospf
     90.0.0.0/24 is subnetted, 1 subnets
O IA    90.10.0.0 [110/3] via 172.16.0.2, 00:12:48, FastEthernet0/1
O IA 192.168.0.0 [110/2] via 172.16.0.2, 00:12:48, FastEthernet0/1
```

```
R3#show ip route ospf
     10.0.0.0/24 is subnetted, 1 subnets
O IA    10.0.1.0 [110/3] via 192.168.0.1, 00:13:47, FastEthernet0/0
O IA 172.16.0.0 [110/2] via 192.168.0.1, 00:13:47, FastEthernet0/0
```

Characters IA in front of the routes indicate that these routes reside in different areas.

> **NOTE**
>
> Since they reside in different areas, R1 and R3 will never establish a neighbor relationship.

Designated & Backup Designated Router

Based on the network type, OSPF router can elect one router to be a Designated Router (DR) and one router to be a Backup Designated Router (BDR). For example, on multiaccess broadcast networks (such as LANs) routers defaults to elect a DR and BDR. DR and BDR serve as the central point for exchanging OSPF routing information. Each non-DR or non-BDR router will exchange routing information only with the DR and BDR, instead of exchanging updates with every router on the network segment. DR will then distribute topology information to every other router inside the same area, which greatly reduces OSPF traffic.

To send routing information to a DR or BDR the multicast address of 224.0.0.6 is used. DR sends routing updates to the multicast address of 224.0.0.5. If DR fails, BDR takes over its role of redistributing routing information.

Every router on a network segment will establish a full neighbor relationship with the DR and BDR. Non-DR and non-BDR routers will establish a two way neighbor relationship between themselves.

> **NOTE**
>
> On point-to-point links, a DR and BDR are not elected since only two routers are directly connected.

On LANs, DR and BDR must be elected. Two rules are used to elect a DR and BDR:

To better understand the concept, consider the following example.

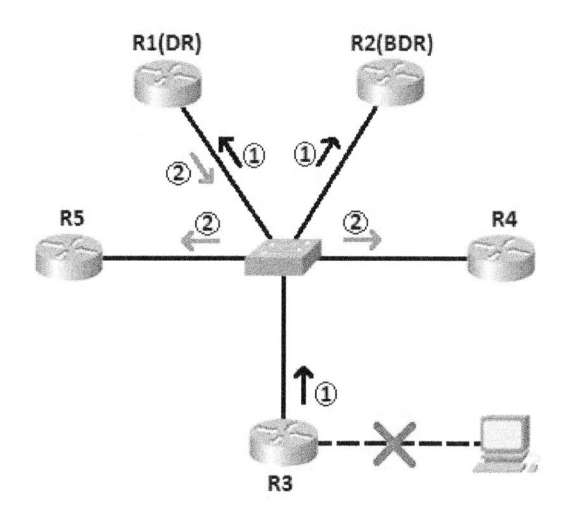

All routers depicted above are in the same area (area 0). All routers are running OSPF. Routers R1 and R2 have been elected as DR and BDR because they have the highest and the second highest router ID (100.0.0.0 and 90.0.0.0 respectively). If, for example, R3's directly connected subnet fails, R3 informs R1 and R2 (the DR and BDR for the segment) of the network change (step 1). R1 then informs all other non-DR and non-BDR routers of the change in topology (step 2).

We can verify that R1 and R2 are indeed the DR and BDR of the segment by typing the show ip ospf neighbors command on R3:

```
R3#show ip ospf neighbor
Neighbor ID   Pri  State          Dead Time  Address    Interface
60.0.0.0      1    FULL/DROTHER   00:00:33   10.0.0.5   FastEthernet0/0
100.0.0.0     1    FULL/DR        00:00:33   10.0.0.1   FastEthernet0/0
70.0.0.0      1    FULL/DROTHER   00:00:33   10.0.0.4   FastEthernet0/0
90.0.0.0      1    FULL/BDR       00:00:33   10.0.0.2   FastEthernet0/0
```

NOTE

You can influence the DR and BDR election process by manually configuring the OSPF priority. This is done by using the ip ospf priority VALUE command interface command.

OSPF authentication

OSPF can be configured to authenticate every OSPF message. This is usually done to prevent a rogue router from injecting false routing information and therefore causing a Denial-of-Service attack.

Two types of authentication can be used:

> NOTE
>
> With OSPF authentication turned on, routers must pass the authentication process before becoming OSPF neighbors.

To configure clear text authentication, the following steps are required:

In the following example, we will configure OSPF clear-text authentication.

```
        R1        area 0        R2
```

Both routers are running OSPF. On R1, we need to enter the following commands:

```
R1(config)#int fa0/0
R1(config-if)#ip ospf authentication-key secret
R1(config-if)#ip ospf authentication
```

The same commands must be entered on R2:

```
R2(config)#int fa0/0
R2(config-if)#ip ospf authentication-key secret
R2(config-if)#ip ospf authentication
```

To verify that clear-text authentication is indeed turned on, we can use the show ip ospf interface *INTERFACE_NUMBER/INTERFACE_TYPE* command on either router:

```
R1#show ip ospf interface fa0/0
FastEthernet0/0 is up, line protocol is up
  Internet address is 10.0.0.1/24, Area 0
  Process ID 1, Router ID 1.1.1.1, Network Type BROADCAST, Cost: 1
  Transmit Delay is 1 sec, State DR, Priority 1
  Designated Router (ID) 1.1.1.1, Interface address 10.0.0.1
  No backup designated router on this network
  Timer intervals configured, Hello 10, Dead 40, Wait 40, Retransmit 5
    Hello due in 00:00:07
  Index 1/1, flood queue length 0
  Next 0x0(0)/0x0(0)
  Last flood scan length is 1, maximum is 1
  Last flood scan time is 0 msec, maximum is 0 msec
  Neighbor Count is 1, Adjacent neighbor count is 1
    Adjacent with neighbor 2.2.2.2
  Suppress hello for 0 neighbor(s)
  Simple password authentication enabled
```

Configuring OSPF MD5 authentication is very similar to configuring clear-text authentication. Two commands are also used:

Here is an example configuration on R1:

```
R1(config)#int fa0/0
R1(config-if)#ip ospf message-digest-key 1 md5 secret
R1(config-if)#ip ospf authentication message-digest
```

You can verify that R1 is using OSPF MD5 authentication by typing the show ip ospf INTERFACE/INTERFACE_TYPE command:

```
R1#show ip ospf interface fa0/0
FastEthernet0/0 is up, line protocol is up
  Internet address is 10.0.0.1/24, Area 0
  Process ID 1, Router ID 1.1.1.1, Network Type BROADCAST, Cost: 1
  Transmit Delay is 1 sec, State DR, Priority 1
  Designated Router (ID) 1.1.1.1, Interface address 10.0.0.1
  No backup designated router on this network
  Timer intervals configured, Hello 10, Dead 40, Wait 40, Retransmit 5
    Hello due in 00:00:02
  Index 1/1, flood queue length 0
  Next 0x0(0)/0x0(0)
  Last flood scan length is 1, maximum is 1
  Last flood scan time is 0 msec, maximum is 0 msec
  Neighbor Count is 1, Adjacent neighbor count is 1
    Adjacent with neighbor 2.2.2.2
  Suppress hello for 0 neighbor(s)
  Message digest authentication enabled
    Youngest key id is 1
```

> **NOTE**
>
> OSPF authentication type can also be enabled on an area basis, instead of configuring OSPF authentication type per interface basis. This is done by using the area AREA_ID authentication [message-digest] command under the OSPF configuration mode. If you omit the message-digest keyword, a clear-text authentication will be used for that area. All interfaces inside the area will use OSPF authentication.

OSPF summarization

Route summarization helps reduce OSPF traffic and route computation. OSPF, unlike EIGRP, doesn't support automatic summarization. Also, unlike EIGRP, where you can summarize routes on every router in an EIGRP network, OSFP can summarize routes only on ABRs and ASBRs.

The following command is used for OSPF summarization:

```
(config-router) area AREA_ID range IP_ADDRESS MASK
```

To better understand OSPF summarization, consider the following example network:

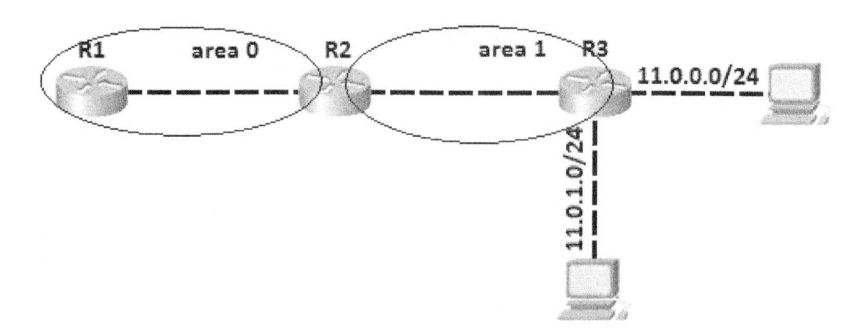

```
    R1    area 0   R2        area 1   R3
                                         11.0.0.0/24


                                      11.0.1.0/24
```

All three routers are running OSPF and exchanging routers. Before OSPF summarization is configured, the router R1 inside the backbone area has two entries for the networks 11.0.0.0/24 and 11.0.1.0/24 in its routing table.

```
         10.0.0.0/24 is subnetted, 1 subnets
C        10.0.0.0 is directly connected, FastEthernet0/0
R1#
R1#
R1#show ip route
Codes: C - connected, S - static, I - IGRP, R - RIP, M - mobile, B - BGP
       D - EIGRP, EX - EIGRP external, O - OSPF, IA - OSPF inter area
       N1 - OSPF NSSA external type 1, N2 - OSPF NSSA external type 2
       E1 - OSPF external type 1, E2 - OSPF external type 2, E - EGP
       i - IS-IS, L1 - IS-IS level-1, L2 - IS-IS level-2, ia - IS-IS inter area
       * - candidate default, U - per-user static route, o - ODR
       P - periodic downloaded static route

Gateway of last resort is not set

         10.0.0.0/24 is subnetted, 1 subnets
C        10.0.0.0 is directly connected, FastEthernet0/0
         11.0.0.0/24 is subnetted, 2 subnets
O IA     11.0.0.0 [110/3] via 10.0.0.2, 00:00:08, FastEthernet0/0
O IA     11.0.1.0 [110/12] via 10.0.0.2, 00:00:08, FastEthernet0/0
O IA  172.16.0.0/16 [110/2] via 10.0.0.2, 00:02:03, FastEthernet0/0
R1#
```

We could summarize these two subnets on R2, so that R1 receive only one routing update for both subnets. To do that, the following command can be used on R2:

```
R2(config)#router ospf 1
R2(config-router)#area 1 range 11.0.0.0 255.255.0.0
```

Now, R1 has only one entry in its routing table for R3's directly connected subnets:

```
     11.0.0.0/16 is subnetted, 1 subnets
O IA    11.0.0.0 [110/2] via 172.16.0.1, 00:00:27, FastEthernet0/0
```

> NOTE
>
> Be careful with summarization. In this case, router R1 thinks that R2 has routes for all subnets in the range 11.0.0.0 – 11.0.255.255. When summarizing, try to be as specific as possible.

OSPF summary

Here is a list of the most important OSPF features:

- link state routing protocol
- classless routing protocol
- supports VLSM (Variable Length Subnet Mask)
- converges fast
- uses the concept of areas
- uses multicast address for routing updates (224.0.0.5 and 224.0.0.6)
- sends partial routing updates
- supports only equal cost load balancing
- manual summarization can be done only on ABRs and ASBRs
- uses interface cost as a metric
- uses SPF algorithm to calculate the best paths
- open standard
- each router inside an area has the same topology table
- supports clear-text and MD5 authentication

Differences between OSPF and EIGRP

The following table lists the differences between OSPF and EIGRP:

Protocol	Type of routing	Metric	Manual summarization	Load balancing	Administrative distance	Cisco proprietary	Multicast address
EIGRP	advanced distance vector	composite of bandwidth and delay	on all routers	equal and unequal cost load balancing	90	Yes	224.0.0.10
OSPF	link state	cost	only on ABRs and ASBRs	equal cost load balancing	110	No	224.0.0.5, 224.0.0.6

Comparing internal routing protocols (IGPs)

The following table lists the differences between the three most popular interior routing protocols:

Feature	RIP	EIGRP	OSPF
Type	distance vector	hybrid	distance vector
Metric	hop count	Bandwidth and delay	cost
Speed of Convergence	slow	fast	fast
Routing	classful (RIPv1) classful (RIPv2)	classless	classless
Updates	Periodical broadcast (RIPv1), multicast (RIPv2)	multicast	multicast
Manual Summarization	No (RIPv1), yes (RIPv2)	yes	yes
Supported on non-Cisco Routers	yes	no	yes
Configuration Complexity	easy	medium	hard

PART VI
LAN SWITCHING

PART VI: LAN Switching

Layer 2 switching

Layer 2 switching (or Data Link layer switching) is the process of using devices' MAC addresses to decide where to forward frames. Switches and bridges are used for Layer 2 switching. They break up one large **collision domain** into multiple smaller ones.

In a typical LAN, all hosts are connected to one central device. In the past, the device was usually a hub. But hubs had many disadvantages, such as not being aware of traffic that passes through them, creating one large collision domain, etc. To overcome some of the problems with hubs, bridges were created. They were better than hubs because they created multiple collision domains, but they had limited number of ports. Finally, switches were created and are still widely used today. Switches have more ports than bridges, can inspect incoming traffic and make forwarding decisions accordingly. Also. each port on a switch is a separate collision domain, so no packet collisions should occur.

Layer 2 switches are faster than routers because they don't take up time looking at the Network layer header information. Instead, they look at the frame's hardware addresses to decide what to do with the frame – to forward, flood, or drop it. Here are other major advantages of Layer 2 switching:

- ❖ fast hardware-based bridging (using ASICs chips)
- ❖ wire speed
- ❖ low latency
- ❖ low cost

Here is an example of the typical LAN network – the switch serves as a central device that connects all devices together:

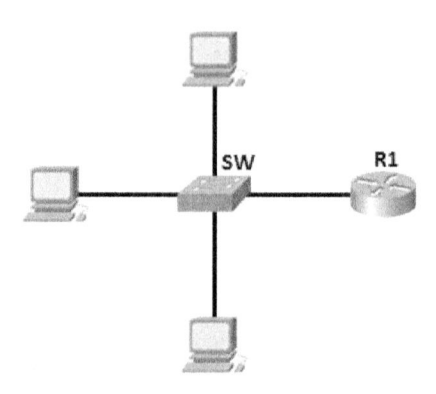

Differences between hubs and switches

To better understand the concept of frame switching based on the hardware address of a device, you need to understand how switches differ from hubs.

First, consider an example of a LAN in which all hosts connects to a hub:

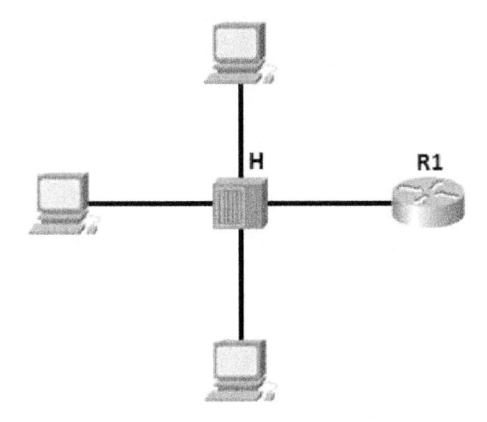

As mentioned previously, hubs create only a single collision domain, so the chance for a collision to occur is high. The hub depicted above simply repeats the signal it receives out all ports, except the one from which the signal was received, so no frame filtering takes place. Imagine if you had 20 hosts connected to a hub, a packet would be sent to 19 hosts, instead of just one! This can also cause security problems, because an attacker can capture all traffic on the network.

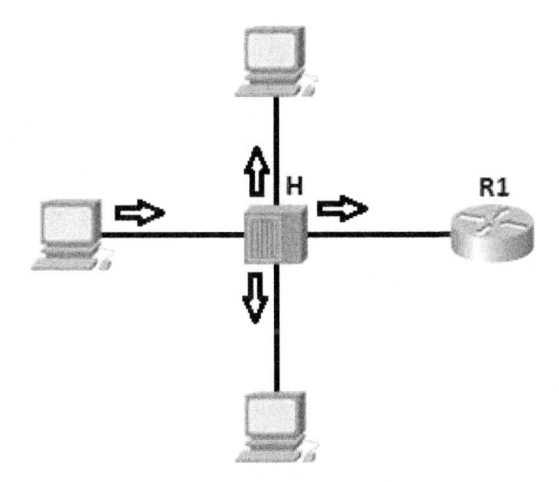

Now consider the way the switches work. We have the same topology as above, only this time we are using a switch instead of a hub:

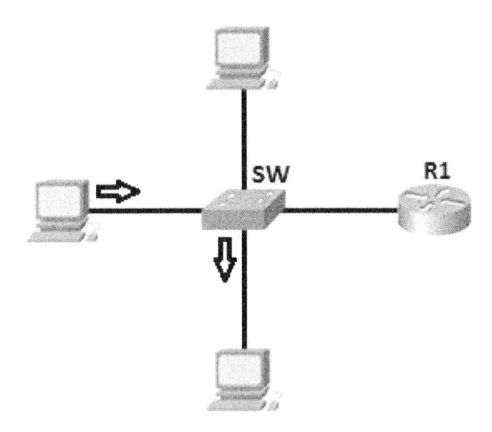

Switches increase the number of collision domains. Each port is one collision domain, which means that the chances for collisions to occur are minimal. A switch learns which device is connected to which port and forwards a frame based on the destination MAC address included in the frame. This reduces traffic on the LAN and enhances security.

How switches work

Each network card has a unique identifier called a Media Access Control (MAC) address. This address is used in LANs for communication between devices on the same network segment. Devices that want to communicate need to know each other MAC addresses before sending out packets.

Switches also use MAC addresses to make accurate forwarding or filtering decision. When a switch receives a frame, it associates the media access control (MAC) address of the sending device with the port on which it was received. The table that stores such associations is called a MAC address table. This table is stored in the volatile memory, so associations are erased after the switch is rebooted.

Switches usually perform these three functions in a LAN:

- ❖ address learning – switches learn MAC addresses by examining the source MAC address of each received frame.
- ❖ forward/filter decisions – switches decide whether to forward or filter a frame, based on the destination MAC address.
- ❖ loop avoidance – switches use **Spanning Tree Protocol (STP)** to prevent network loops while still permitting redundancy.

86

To better how a network switch works, take a look at the following example:

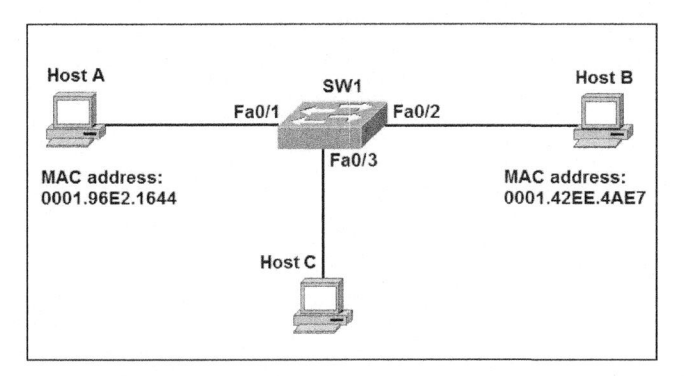

```
Host A                    SW1                    Host B
             Fa0/1               Fa0/2
                        Fa0/3
MAC address:                              MAC address:
0001.96E2.1644                            0001.42EE.4AE7

                        Host C
```

Let's say that host A wants to communicate with host B for the first time. Host A knows the IP address of host B, but since this is the first time the two hosts communicate, the hardware (MAC) addresses are not known. Host A uses the **ARP process** to find out the MAC address of host B. The switch forwards the ARP request out all ports except the port the host A is connected to. Host B receives the ARP request and responds with its MAC address. Host B also learns the MAC address of host A (because host A sent its MAC address in the ARP request). Host C receives the ARP request, but doesn't respond since the IP address listed in the request is not its own.

As mentioned above, a switch learns which MAC addresses are associated with which port by examining the source MAC address of each received frame. Because host B responded with the ARP reply that included its MAC address, the switch knows the MAC address of host B and stores that address in its MAC address table. For host A, the switch knows its MAC address because of the ARP request that included it.

Now, when host A sends a packet to host B, the switch looks up in its MAC address table and forwards the frame only out the Fa0/2 port – the port on which host B is connected to. Other hosts on the network will not be involved in the communication:

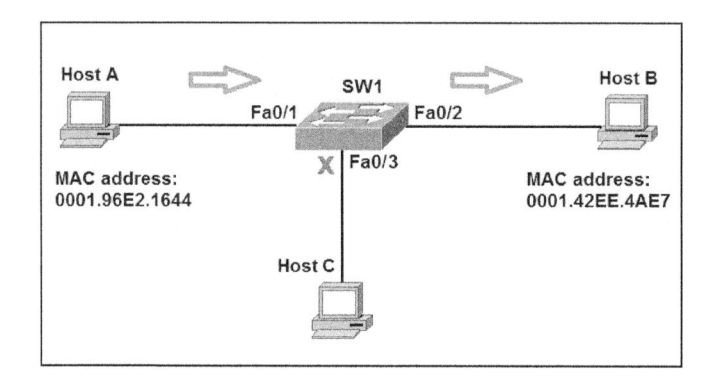

```
                   Host A                  SW1                    Host B
                            Fa0/1              Fa0/2
                                      X  Fa0/3
                   MAC address:                            MAC address:
                   0001.96E2.1644                          0001.42EE.4AE7

                                         Host C
```

> NOTE
>
> By default, MAC addresses stay in the switch's MAC address table for 5 minutes. So if host A and host B decide to communicate inside the next 5 minutes, a new ARP process will not be necessary.

You can display the MAC address table of the switch by using the show mac-address-table command:

```
SW1#show mac-address-table
          Mac Address Table
-------------------------------------------

Vlan    Mac Address       Type        Ports
----    -----------       --------    -----
   1    0001.42ee.4ae7    DYNAMIC     Fa0/2
   1    0001.96e2.1644    DYNAMIC     Fa0/1
```

The output is pretty much self-explanatory: all ports belong to VLAN 1 and MAC addresses associated with specific ports are listed. **DYNAMIC** means that the address was learned dynamically by using the source MAC address of the received frames.

Collision & broadcast domain

Collision domain

A collision domain is, as the name implies, the part of a network where packet collisions can occur. A collision occurs when two devices send a packet at the same time on the shared network segment. The packets collide and both devices must send the packets again, which reduces network efficiency. Collisions are often in a hub environment, because each port on a hub is in the same collision domain. By contrast, each port on a bridge, a switch or a router is in a separate collision domain.

The following example illustrates collision domains:

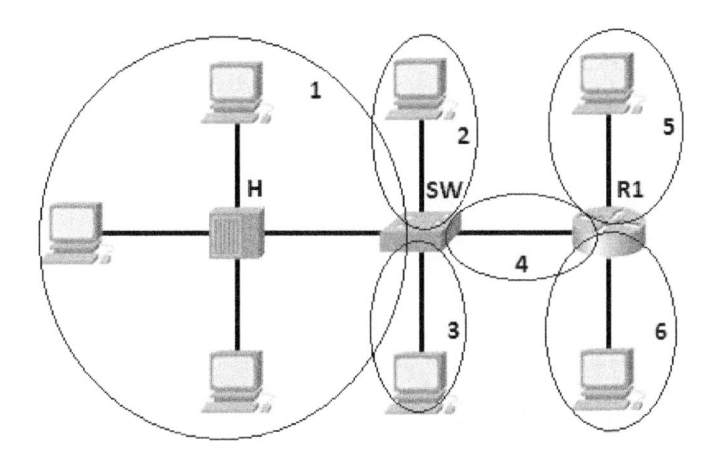

We have 6 collision domains in the example above.

> NOTE
>
> Remember, each port on a hub is in the same collision domain. Each port on a bridge, a switch or router is in a separate collision domain.

Broadcast domain

A broadcast domain is the domain in which a broadcast is forwarded. A broadcast domain contains all devices that can reach each other at the data link layer (OSI layer 2) by using broadcast. All ports on a hub or a switch are by default in the same broadcast domain. All ports on a router are in the different broadcast domains and routers don't forward broadcasts from one broadcast domain to another.

89

The following example clarifies the concept:

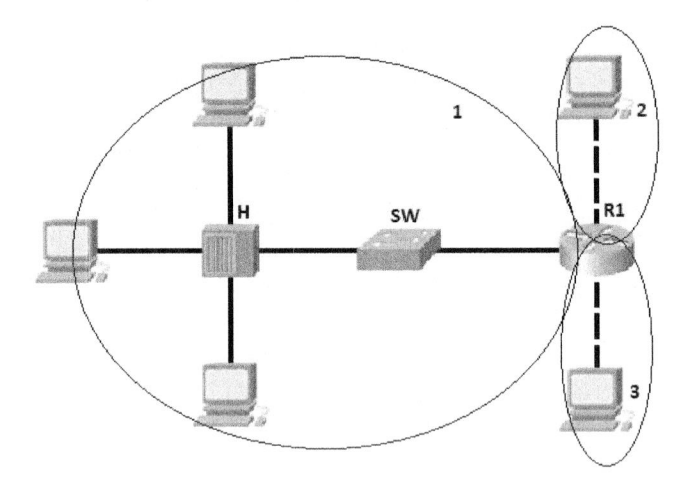

In the picture above we have three broadcast domains, since all ports on a hub or a switch are in the same broadcast domain, and all ports on a router are in a different broadcast domain.

CSMA/CD

CSMA/CD (Carrier Sense Multiple Access with Collision Detection) helps hosts to decide when to send packets on a shared network segment and how to detect collisions if they occur. For example, in a hub network, two devices can send packets at the same time. This can cause a collision. CSMA/CD enables devices to "sense" the wire to ensure that no other device is currently transmitting packets. But, if two devices "sense" that the wire is clear and send packets at the same time, a collision can occur. If the collision occurs, packets have to be resent after a random period of time.

Consider the following example:

90

```
              Host C
                 🖥
                 ⬇

  Host A                    Host B
     🖥                        🖥
         ➡     ▣  ✗
                  collision


              Host D
                 🖥
```

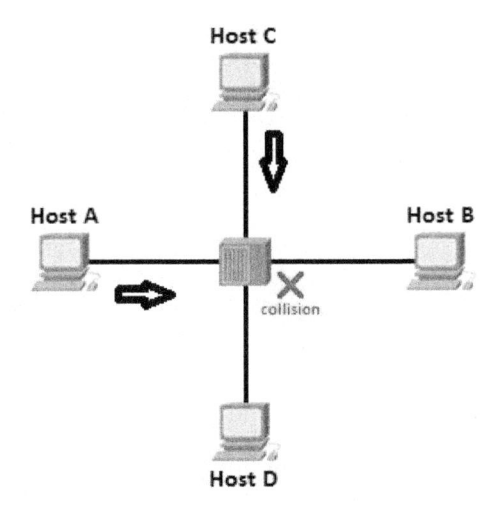

In the topology above we have a hub network. Host A is trying to communicate with host B. Host A "senses" the wire and decides to send packets. But, in the same time, host C sends its packets to host D and the collision occurs. The sending devices (host A and host C) detect the collision and resend the packet after a random period of time.

> **NOTE**
>
> Since switches are now commonly used in networks instead of hubs, CSMA/CD is not really used anymore. Each port on a switch usually operate in a full duplex mode and there are no packet collisions in a full duplex mode.

PART VII: VLAN

What is a VLAN?

VLANs (Virtual LANs) are logical grouping of devices in the same broadcast domain. VLANs are usually configured on switches by placing some interfaces into one broadcast domain and some interfaces into another. Each VLAN acts as a subgroup of the switch ports in an Ethernet LAN.

VLANs can spread across multiple switches, with each VLAN being treated as its own subnet or broadcast domain. This means that frames broadcasted onto the network will be switched only between the ports within the same VLAN.

A VLAN acts like a physical LAN, but it allows hosts to be grouped together in the same broadcast domain even if they are not connected to the same switch. Here are the main reasons why VLANs are used:

- ❖ VLANs increase the number of broadcast domains while decreasing their size.
- ❖ VLANs reduce security risks by reducing the number of hosts that receive copies of frames that the switches flood.
- ❖ you can keep hosts that hold sensitive data on a separate VLAN to improve security.
- ❖ you can create more flexible network designs that group users by department instead of by physical location.
- ❖ network changes are achieved with ease by just configuring a port into the appropriate VLAN.

The following topology shows a network with all hosts inside the same VLAN:

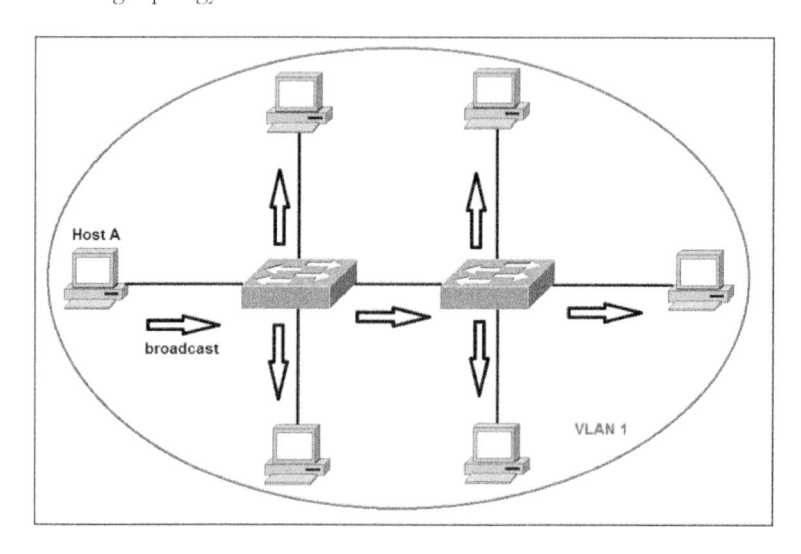

Without VLANs, a broadcast sent from host A would reach all devices on the network. Each device will receive and process broadcast frames, increasing the CPU overhead on each device and reducing the overall security of the network.

By placing interfaces on both switches into a separate VLAN, a broadcast from host A would reach only devices inside the same VLAN, since each VLAN is a separate broadcast domain. Hosts in other VLANs will not even be aware that the communication took place. This is shown in the picture below:

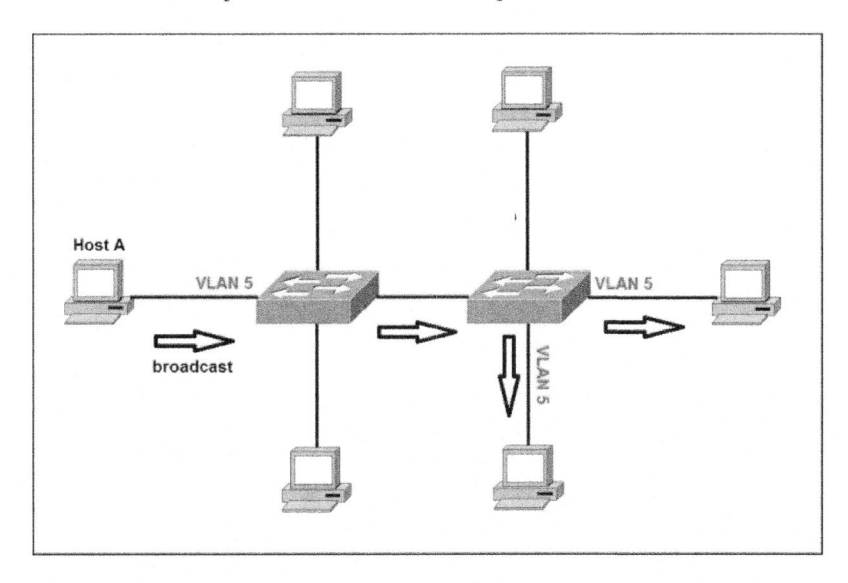

NOTE

To reach hosts in a different VLAN, a router is needed.

Access and trunk ports

If you intend to use VLANs in your network, you will need to configure some ports on a switch as access ports and other as trunk ports. Here is a description each port type:

- ❖ access port – a port that can be assigned to a single VLAN. This type of interface is configured on switch ports that are connected to end devices such as workstations, printers, or access points.
- ❖ trunk port – a port that is connected to another switch. This type of interface can carry traffic of multiple VLANs, thus enabling you to extend VLANs across your entire network. Frames are tagged by assigning a VLAN ID to each frame as they traverse between switches.

The following picture illustrates the difference:

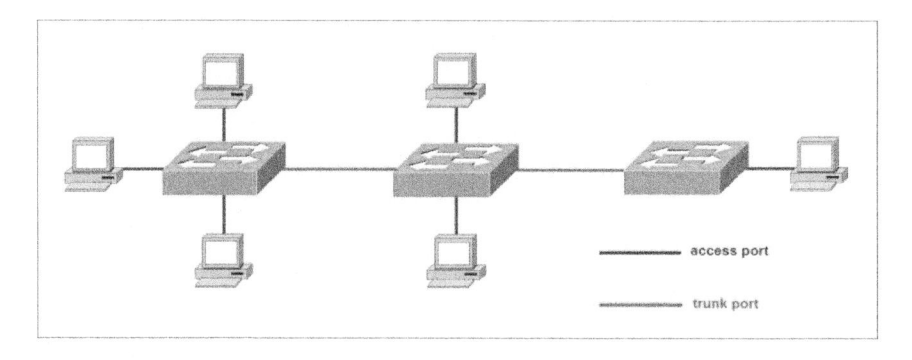

In the example network pictured above, the switch ports connected to workstations would be configured as access ports. The ports that connect switches together would be configured as trunk ports.

Configuring VLANs

By default, all ports on a switch are in the VLAN 1. We can verify that by typing the show vlan command from the IOS enable mode of a switch:

```
Switch#show vlan

VLAN Name                             Status    Ports
---- -------------------------------- --------- -------------------------------
1    default                          active    Fa0/1, Fa0/2, Fa0/3, Fa0/4
                                                Fa0/5, Fa0/6, Fa0/7, Fa0/8
                                                Fa0/9, Fa0/10, Fa0/11, Fa0/12
                                                Fa0/13, Fa0/14, Fa0/15, Fa0/16
                                                Fa0/17, Fa0/18, Fa0/19, Fa0/20
                                                Fa0/21, Fa0/22, Fa0/23, Fa0/24
1002 fddi-default                     act/unsup
1003 token-ring-default               act/unsup
1004 fddinet-default                  act/unsup
1005 trnet-default                    act/unsup

VLAN Type  SAID       MTU   Parent RingNo BridgeNo Stp  BrdgMode Trans1 Trans2
---- ----- ---------- ----- ------ ------ -------- ---- -------- ------ ------
1    enet  100001     1500  -      -      -        -    -        0      0
1002 fddi  101002     1500  -      -      -        -    -        0      0
1003 tr    101003     1500  -      -      -        -    -        0      0
1004 fdnet 101004     1500  -      -      -        ieee -        0      0
1005 trnet 101005     1500  -      -      -        ibm  -        0      0

Remote SPAN VLANs
------------------------------------------------------------------------------


Primary Secondary Type              Ports
```

In the picture above, you can see that all of the 24 ports of the switch are in the same VLAN, namely VLAN 1.

Two steps are required to create a VLAN and assign a switch port to the VLAN:

Here is an example of assigning the VLAN 2 to the interface:

```
Switch(config)#vlan 2
Switch(config-vlan)#exit
Switch(config)#int fa0/1
Switch(config-if)#switchport mode access
Switch(config-if)#switchport access vlan 2
```

The first command (*vlan 2*) created the VLAN 2. We've then entered the Fa0/1 subinterface mode and configured the interface as an access interface that belongs to VLAN 2. To verify this, we can again use the show vlan command:

```
Switch#show vlan

VLAN Name                             Status    Ports
---- -------------------------------- --------- -------------------------------
1    default                          active    Fa0/2, Fa0/3, Fa0/4, Fa0/5
                                                Fa0/6, Fa0/7, Fa0/8, Fa0/9
                                                Fa0/10, Fa0/11, Fa0/12, Fa0/13
                                                Fa0/14, Fa0/15, Fa0/16, Fa0/17
                                                Fa0/18, Fa0/19, Fa0/20, Fa0/21
                                                Fa0/22, Fa0/23, Fa0/24
2    VLAN0002                         active    Fa0/1
1002 fddi-default                     act/unsup
1003 token-ring-default               act/unsup
1004 fddinet-default                  act/unsup
1005 trnet-default                    act/unsup

VLAN Type  SAID       MTU   Parent RingNo BridgeNo Stp  BrdgMode Trans1 Trans2
---- ----- ---------- ----- ------ ------ -------- ---- -------- ------ ------
1    enet  100001     1500  -      -      -        -    -        0      0
2    enet  100002     1500  -      -      -        -    -        0      0
1002 fddi  101002     1500  -      -      -        -    -        0      0
1003 tr    101003     1500  -      -      -        -    -        0      0
1004 fdnet 101004     1500  -      -      -        ieee -        0      0
1005 trnet 101005     1500  -      -      -        ibm  -        0      0

Remote SPAN VLANs
------------------------------------------------------------------------------


Primary Secondary Type              Ports
```

Configuring access & trunk ports

To configure an interface to be an access interface, the switchport mode access interface command is used. This type of interface can be assigned only to a single VLAN.

To configure a trunk interface, the switchport mode trunk interface command is used. This type of interface can carry traffic of multiple VLANs.

An example will help you understand the concept.

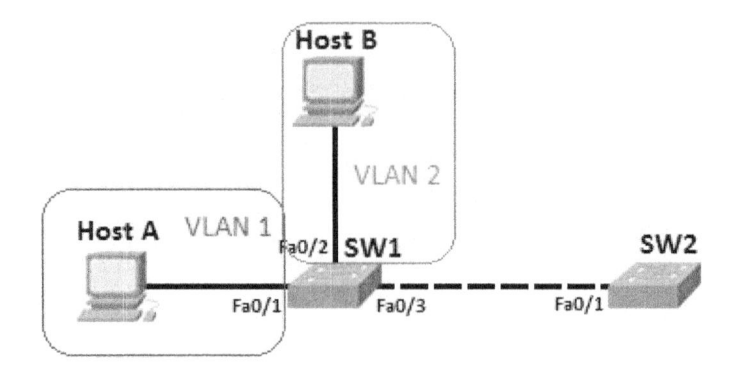

Host A and host B are in different VLANs, VLAN 1 and VLAN 2. These ports need to be configured as access ports and assigned to their respective VLANs by using the following sequence of commands:

```
SW1(config)#int fa0/1
SW1(config-if)#switchport mode access
SW1(config-if)#exit
SW1(config)#vlan 2
SW1(config-vlan)#exit
SW1(config)#int fa0/2
SW1(config-if)#switchport mode access
SW1(config-if)#switchport access vlan 2
SW1(config-if)#
```

Because the link between SW1 and SW2 needs to carry traffic of multiple VLANs, it needs to be configured as a trunk interface. This is done by using the following commands on both SW1 and SW2:

On SW1:

```
SW1(config)#int fa0/3
SW1(config-if)#switchport mode trunk
```

On SW2:

```
SW2(config)#int fa0/1
SW2(config-if)#switchport mode trunk
```

Now the link between SW1 and SW2 can carry traffic from both the VLAN1 and VLAN2. You can verify that an interface is indeed a trunk interface by using the show interface Fa0/3 switchport command on SW1:

```
SW1#show interface fa0/3 switchport
Name: Fa0/3
Switchport: Enabled
Administrative Mode: trunk
Operational Mode: trunk
Administrative Trunking Encapsulation: dot1q
Operational Trunking Encapsulation: dot1q
Negotiation of Trunking: On
Access Mode VLAN: 1 (default)
Trunking Native Mode VLAN: 1 (default)
Voice VLAN: none
Administrative private-vlan host-association: none
Administrative private-vlan mapping: none
Administrative private-vlan trunk native VLAN: none
Administrative private-vlan trunk encapsulation: dot1q
Administrative private-vlan trunk normal VLANs: none
Administrative private-vlan trunk private VLANs: none
Operational private-vlan: none
Trunking VLANs Enabled: ALL
Pruning VLANs Enabled: 2-1001
Capture Mode Disabled
Capture VLANs Allowed: ALL
Protected: false
Appliance trust: none
SW1#
```

NOTE

VLAN 1 doesn't have to be created, it exists by default. Also, by default, all ports are in the VLAN 1, so Fa0/1 doesn't need the switchport access vlan 1 command.

Frame tagging

To identify the VLAN a packet is belonging to, switches use tagging to assign a numerical value to each frame in a network with multiple VLANs. This is done to ensure that switches know out which ports to forward frames.

For example, consider the following network topology.

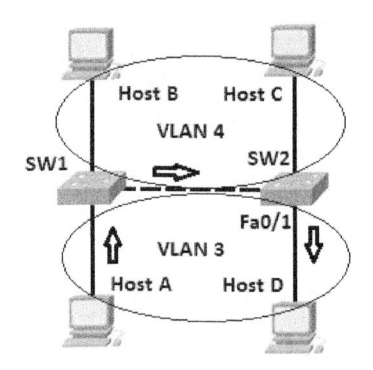

There are two VLANs in the topology pictured above, namely VLAN 3 and VLAN 4. Host A sends a broadcast packet to switch SW1. Switch SW1 receives the packet, tags the packet with the VLAN ID of 3 and sends it to SW2. SW2 receives the packet, looks up at the VLAN ID, and forwards the packet only out the port Fa0/1, since only that port is in VLAN 3. Host B and host C will not receive the packet because they are in different VLAN than host A.

> NOTE
>
> When forwarding a tagged frame to a host device a switch will remove the VLAN tag, since host devices don't understand tagging and would drop the packet.

IEEE 802.1Q

IEEE 802.1Q is one of the VLAN tagging protocols supported by Cisco switches. This standard was created by the Institute of Electrical and Electronics Engineers (IEEE), so it an open standard and can be used on non-Cisco switches.

To identify to which VLAN a frame belongs to, a field is inserted into the frame's header.

Original frame:

| Destination MAC | Source MAC | Length/Type | Data | FCS |

802.1Q frame:

| Destination MAC | 802.1Q Tag | Source MAC | Length/Type | Data | FCS |

An example will attempt to clarify the concept. Let's say that we have a network of 2 switches and 4 hosts. Hosts A and host D are in VLAN 2, while hosts B and C are in VLAN 3.

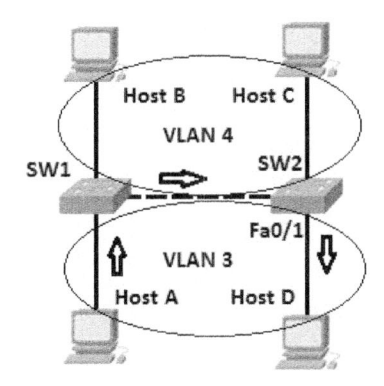

On the segment between two switches, a process called VLAN trunking is used. Let's say that host A sends a broadcast frame. SW1 "tags" the frame by inserting the VLAN ID in the header of the frame before sending the frame to SW2. SW2 receives the frame and knows that the frame belongs to VLAN 3, so it sends the frame only to host D, since that host is in VLAN 3.

Inter-Switch Link (ISL)

Another VLAN tagging protocol is Inter-Switch Link (ISL). This protocol is Cisco proprietary, which means that, unlike 802.1Q, it can be used only between Cisco switches. It is considered to be deprecated, and newer Cisco switches don't even support it.

ISL works by encapsulating a frame in an ISL header and trailer. The encapsulated frame remains unchanged. The VLAN ID is included in the ISL header.

Original frame:

Destination MAC	Source MAC	Length/Type	Data	FCS

ISL frame:

ISL Header	Destination MAC	Source MAC	Length/Type	Data	FCS	ISL FCS

Configuring voice VLANs

Most corporate networks today use IP telephony. This means that the phones are connect to the same network and use the same cabling as other network devices, such as workstations or routers. Since offices usually have only a single UTP cable to each desk, most of the IP phones today include a small switch that enable you to connect your PC to the phone sitting on the desk, and then connect the phone to the local network.

Consider the backside of an IP telephone Yealink T21:

As you can see from the picture, this phone has two UTP ports. One port is connected to the local network, while the other port can be connected to the PC.

The port on the phone connected to the switch can carry both data and voice traffic. To enable this, we need to define two VLANs on the switch port – data VLAN and voice VLAN. Here is how we can do that

```
SW1(config)#vlan 5
SW1(config)#vlan 20
SW1(config)#int fa0/1
SW1(config-if)#switchport mode access
SW1(config-if)#switchport access vlan 5
SW1(config-if)#switchport voice vlan 20
```

We've created two VLANs – VLAN 5 that will be used for data sent by the PC and VLAN 20 for IP phone's voice traffic. We've then placed the port into both VLANs. The keyword voice indicates that the VLAN 20 will be a voice VLAN.

To verify that the interface indeed carries data from both VLANs, we can use the show interfaces Fa0/1 switchport command:

```
Switch#show interfaces fa0/1 switchport
Name: Fa0/1
Switchport: Enabled
Administrative Mode: static access
Operational Mode: static access
Administrative Trunking Encapsulation: dot1q
Operational Trunking Encapsulation: native
Negotiation of Trunking: Off
Access Mode VLAN: 5 (VLAN0005)
Trunking Native Mode VLAN: 1 (default)
```

> Voice VLAN: 20
> Administrative private-vlan host-association: none
> Administrative private-vlan mapping: none
> ...

The lines Access Mode VLAN: 5 (VLAN0005) and Voice VLAN: 20 indicate that the interface is indeed carrying traffic from both VLANs.

> NOTE
>
> Some IP phones can be automatically configured with appropriate VLANs using protocols such as LLDP or CDP. However, on some models you will need to manually configure data and voice VLANs on the phone using its web interface.

Configuring allowed VLANs

By default, all VLANs are allowed across a trunk link on a Cisco switch. We can verify that using the show interfaces trunk command:

> SW1#show interfaces trunk
> Port   Mode   Encapsulation Status   Native vlan
> Fa0/1   on   802.1q   trunking   1
> Port   Vlans allowed on trunk
> Fa0/1   1-1005
> Port   Vlans allowed and active in management domain
> Fa0/1   1,5,10
> Port   Vlans in spanning tree forwarding state and not pruned
> Fa0/1   1,5,10

In the output above you can see that all VLANs (1 through 1005) are allowed on the trunk by default.

We can prevent traffic from certain VLANs from traversing a trunk link using the following interface mode command:

> (config-if)#switchport trunk allowed vlan {add | all | except | remove} vlan-list

For example, to prevent traffic from VLAN 5 to traverse the trunk link, we would use the following command:

> SW1(config)#int fa0/1
> SW1(config-if)#switchport trunk allowed vlan remove 5

The same command needs to be entered on the switch on the other end of the link.

To verify that the traffic from VLAN 5 will indeed be blocked from traversing a trunked link, we can enter the show interfaces trunk command again

```
SW1#show interfaces trunk
Port      Mode       Encapsulation Status      Native vlan
Fa0/1     on         802.1q        trunking    1
Port      Vlans allowed on trunk
Fa0/1     1-4,6-1005
Port      Vlans allowed and active in management domain
Fa0/1     1,10
Port      Vlans in spanning tree forwarding state and not pruned
Fa0/1     none
```

Notice how now only VLANs 1-4 and 6-1005 are allowed on trunk.

> **NOTE**
>
> You can use the switchport trunk allowed vlan all interface mode command to reset the switch port to its original default setting (permitting all VLANs on the trunk).

PART VIII: VTP

What is VTP?

VTP (VLAN Trunking Protocol) is a Cisco proprietary protocol used by Cisco switches to exchange VLAN information. With VTP, you can synchronize VLAN information (such as VLAN ID or VLAN name) with switches inside the same VTP domain. A VTP domain is a set of trunked switches with the matching VTP settings (the domain name, password and VTP version). All switches inside the same VTP domain share their VLAN information with each other.

To better understand the true value of VTP, consider an example network with 100 switches. Without VTP, if you want to create a VLAN on each switch, you will have to manually enter VLAN configuration commands on every switch! VTP enables you to create the VLAN only on a single switch. That switch can then propagate information about the VLAN to every other switch on the network and cause other switches to create it. Likewise, if you want to delete a VLAN, you only need to delete it on one switch, and the change is automatically propagated to every other switch inside the same VTP domain.

The following network topology explains the concept more thoroughly:

On SW1, we have created a new VLAN. SW1 sends a VTP update about the new VLAN to SW2, which in turn sends its VTP update to SW3. These updates will cause SW2 and SW3 to create the same VLAN. You can see how this simplifies network administration – the engineer only had to log in and create the VLAN on the first switch. Other switches have created the same VLAN automatically.

> NOTE
>
> VTP does not advertise information about which switch ports are assigned to which VLAN.

Three VTP versions are available – V1, V2, and V3. The first two versions are similar except that V2 adds support for token ring VLANs. V3 adds the following features:

- ❖ enhanced authentication
- ❖ support for extended VLANs (1006 to 4094). VTP versions 1 and 2 can propagate only VLANs 1 to 1005.

- support for private VLAN
- VTP primary server and VTP secondary servers
- VTP mode off that disables VTP
- backward compatibility with VTP V1 and V2
- the ability to be configured on a per-port basis

VTP modes

Each switch can use one of four different VTP modes:

- VTP client mode – a switch using this mode can't change its VLAN configuration. That means that a VTP client switch cannot create or delete VLANs. However, received VTP updates are processed and forwarded.
- VTP server mode – a switch using this mode can create and delete VLANs. A VTP server switch will propagate VLAN changes. This is the default mode for Cisco switches.
- VTP transparent mode – a switch using this mode doesn't share its VLAN database, but it forwards received VTP advertisements. You can create and delete VLANs on a VTP transparent switch, but these changes will not be sent to other switches.
- VTP mode off – similar to VTP transparent mode, with a difference that a switch using this mode will not forward received VTP updates. This command is supported only in VTP V3.

As mentioned above, all switches are configured as VTP servers by default. This is fine in smaller networks without too many VLANs and VLAN changes, since all VLAN information can easily be stored in each switch's NVRAM. However, in larger networks, it is recommended to specify a couple of higher-quality switches to serve as VTP servers. All other switches in the network should be set up as VTP clients.

Consider the following example:

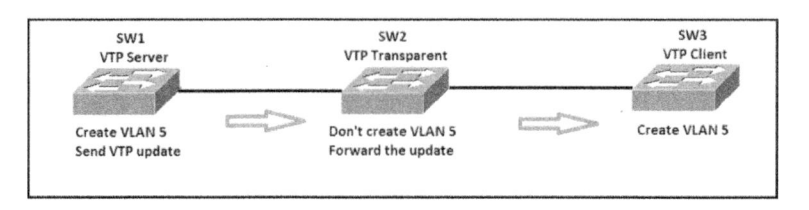

SW1 VTP Server	SW2 VTP Transparent	SW3 VTP Client
Create VLAN 5 Send VTP update	Don't create VLAN 5 Forward the update	Create VLAN 5

We have a simple network of three switches. SW1 is configured as VTP server. After the VLAN 5 is created on SW1, this switch will notify the connected switch (SW2) about the created VLAN. SW2 will receive the update but, since it uses the VTP transparent mode, it will not create this VLAN in its configuration. However, it will forward the VTP update to SW3. Since SW3 is configured as VTP client, it will process the update and create VLAN 5.

VTP configuration

We've already learned that using VTP makes it is possible to make configuration changes on one or more switches and have those changes automatically advertised to all the other switches in the same VTP domain. In a typical network some switches are configured as VTP servers and other switches are configured as VTP clients. A VLAN created on a VTP server switch is automatically advertised to all switches inside the same VTP domain.

> NOTE
>
> With VTP V1 and V2 it is not possible to completely disable VTP on Cisco switches; the best you can do is to place the switch in the VTP transparent mode. VTP V3 adds the mode off option which effectively disables VTP. This article describes the configuration of VTP V1 or V2.

To exchange VTP messages, five requirements must be met:

Consider the following example network:

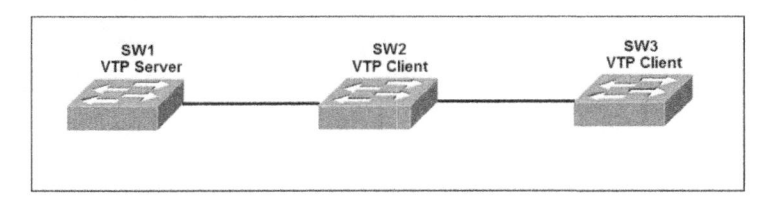

We have a network of three switches connected via trunk links. On SW1, we will configure the VTP domain name using the vtp domain NAME command and VTP password using the vtp password PASSWORD commands:

```
SW1(config)#vtp domain geek
Changing VTP domain name from NULL to geek
SW1(config)#vtp password university
Setting device VLAN database password to university
```

> NOTE
>
> The default VTP mode on Cisco switches is the server mode, so the command vtp mode server wasn't necessary in the SW1 configuration pictured above.

Now we need to configure SW2 and SW3 as VTP clients. We can do it using the following set of commands:

```
SW2(config)#vtp mode client
Setting device to VTP CLIENT mode.
SW2(config)#vtp domain geek
Changing VTP domain name from NULL to geek
SW2(config)#vtp password university
Setting device VLAN database password to university
```

```
SW3(config)#vtp mode client
Setting device to VTP CLIENT mode.
SW3(config)#vtp domain geek
Changing VTP domain name from NULL to geek
SW3(config)#vtp password university
Setting device VLAN database password to university
```

Now, when we create a new VLAN on SW1, the VTP will be sent to SW2 and SW3 and the new VLAN will be created automatically on SW2 and SW3:

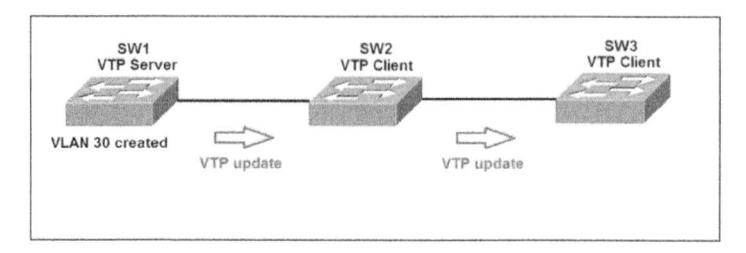

On SW1, we will create a new VLAN:

```
SW1(config)#vlan 30
```

SW2 and SW3 will create the VLAN 30 automatically. We can use the show vlan command on both switches to verify this:

SW2:

```
SW2#show vlan
VLAN Name                 Status    Ports
---- -------------------- --------- -------------------------------
1    default              active    Fa0/3, Fa0/4, Fa0/6, Fa0/7
                                    Fa0/8, Fa0/9, Fa0/10, Fa0/11
                                    Fa0/12, Fa0/13, Fa0/14, Fa0/15
                                    Fa0/16, Fa0/17, Fa0/18, Fa0/19
                                    Fa0/20, Fa0/21, Fa0/22, Fa0/23
                                    Fa0/24
2    Accounting           active    Fa0/5
30   VLAN0030             active
1002 fddi-default         act/unsup
1003 token-ring-default   act/unsup
1004 fddinet-default      act/unsup
1005 trnet-default        act/unsup
```

SW3:

```
SW3#show vlan
VLAN Name                             Status    Ports
---- -------------------------------- --------- -------------------------------
1    default                          active    Fa0/2, Fa0/3, Fa0/4, Fa0/5
                                                Fa0/6, Fa0/7, Fa0/8, Fa0/9
                                                Fa0/10, Fa0/11, Fa0/12, Fa0/13
                                                Fa0/14, Fa0/15, Fa0/16, Fa0/17
                                                Fa0/18, Fa0/19, Fa0/20, Fa0/21
                                                Fa0/22, Fa0/23, Fa0/24
2    Accounting                       active
30   VLAN0030                         active
1002 fddi-default                     act/unsup
1003 token-ring-default               act/unsup
1004 fddinet-default                  act/unsup
1005 trnet-default                    act/unsup
```

To display the VTP configuration information, we can use the show vtp status command:

```
SW3#show vtp status
VTP Version                     : 2
Configuration Revision          : 3
Maximum VLANs supported locally : 255
Number of existing VLANs        : 7
VTP Operating Mode              : Client
VTP Domain Name                 : geek
VTP Pruning Mode                : Disabled
VTP V2 Mode                     : Disabled
VTP Traps Generation            : Disabled
MD5 digest                      : 0x3C 0x8E 0x73 0x0C 0x7D 0x45 0xB6 0xDD
Configuration last modified by 0.0.0.0 at 3-1-93 00:16:02
```

The most important field listed in the output above is the Configuration Revision number. This number indicates the level of revision for a VTP packet. Each device tracks the VTP configuration revision number that is assigned to it. This information is used in order to determine whether the received information is more recent than the current version.

Each time you make a VLAN change on a VTP server, the configuration revision number is incremented by one and a VTP advertisement is sent. The switch that receives a VTP packet compares the configuration revision to its own revision. If the configuration revision number in the received VTP advertisement is higher than its own revision number, the switch will overwrite its VLAN configurations with the new information that is being advertised.

> NOTE
>
> It is important to check a new switch's VTP configuration revision number before adding it to your network. If the revision number on the new switch is higher than the current revision number of other switches on the network, all current VLANs could be deleted!

PART IX: NAT

What is NAT?

NAT (Network Address Translation) is a process of changing the source and destination IP addresses and ports. Address translation reduces the need for IPv4 public addresses and hides private network address ranges. This process is usually done by routers or firewalls.

An example will help you understand the concept:

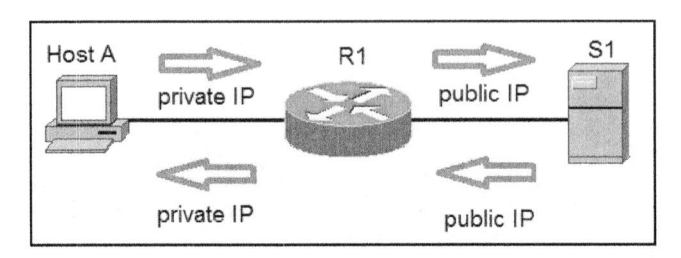

Host A request a web page from an Internet server. Because Host A uses private IP addressing, the source address of the request must be changed by the router because private IP addresses are not routable on the Internet. Router R1 receives the request, changes the source IP address to its public IP address and sends the packet to server S1. Server S1 receives the packet and replies to router R1. Router R1 receives the packet, changes the destination IP addresses to the private IP address of Host A and sends the packet to Host A.

There are three types of address translation:

Static NAT

With static NAT, routers or firewalls translate one private IP address to a single public IP address. Each private IP address is mapped to a single public IP address. Static NAT is not often used because it requires one public IP address for each private IP address.

To configure static NAT, three steps are required:

Here is an example.

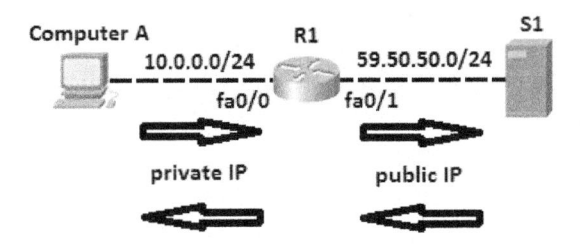

```
                Computer A              R1              S1
                       10.0.0.0/24           59.50.50.0/24
                            fa0/0      fa0/1

                           private IP       public IP
```

Computer A requests a web resource from S1. Computer A uses its private IP address when sending the request to router R1. Router R1 receives the request, changes the private IP address to the public one and sends the request to S1. S1 responds to R1. R1 receives the response, looks up in its NAT table and changes the destination IP address to the private IP address of Computer A.

In the example above, we need to configure static NAT. To do that, the following commands are required on R1:

```
R1(config)#ip nat inside source static 10.0.0.2 59.50.50.1
R1(config)#int fa0/0
R1(config-if)#ip nat inside
R1(config-if)#int fa0/1
R1(config-if)#ip nat outside
```

Using the commands above, we have configured a static mapping between Computer A's private IP address of 10.0.0.2 and router's R1 public IP address of 59.50.50.1. To check NAT, you can use the show ip nat translations command:

```
R1#show ip nat translations
Pro   Inside global     Inside local      Outside local     Outside global
icmp  59.50.50.1:9      10.0.0.2:9        59.50.50.2:9      59.50.50.2:9
---   59.50.50.1        10.0.0.2          ---               ---
```

Dynamic NAT

Unlike with static NAT, where you had to manually define a static mapping between a private and public address, dynamic NAT does the mapping of a local address to a global address happens dynamically. This means that the router dynamically picks an address from the global address pool that is not currently assigned. The dynamic entry stays in the NAT translations table as long as the traffic is exchanged. The entry times out after a period of inactivity and the global IP address can be used for new translations.

With dynamic NAT, you need to specify two sets of addresses on your Cisco router:

- the inside addresses that will be translated
- a pool of global addresses

To configure dynamic NAT, the following steps are required:

Consider the following example:

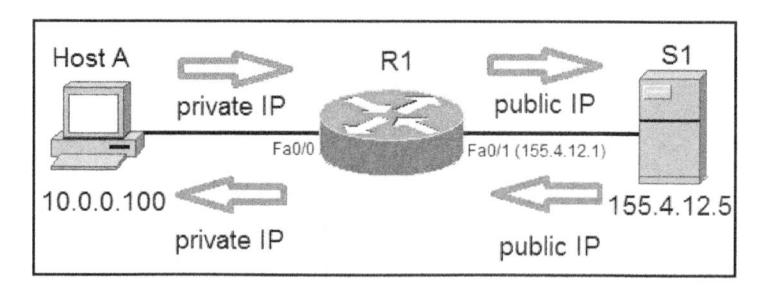

```
Host A                    R1                    S1
        private IP              public IP
              Fa0/0          Fa0/1 (155.4.12.1)
10.0.0.100                                      155.4.12.5
        private IP              public IP
```

Host A requests a web resource from an internet server S1. Host A uses its private IP address when sending the request to router R1. Router R1 receives the request, changes the private IP address to one of the available global addresses in the pool and sends the request to S1. S1 responds to R1. R1 receives the response, looks up in its NAT table and changes the destination IP address to the private IP address of Host A.

To configure dynamic NAT, the following commands are required on R1:

```
R1(config)#int fa0/0
R1(config-if)#ip nat inside
R1(config-if)#int fa0/1
R1(config-if)#ip nat outside
```

```
R1(config)#access-list 1 permit 10.0.0.100 0.0.0.0
```

The access list configured above matches only the 10.0.0.100 IP address.

```
R1(config)#ip nat pool MY_POOL 155.4.12.1 155.4.12.3 netmask 255.255.255.0
```

The pool configured above consists of 3 addresses: 155.4.12.1, 155.4.12.2, and 155.4.12.3.

```
R1(config)#ip nat inside source list 1 pool MY_POOL
```

The command above tells the router to translate all addresses specified in the access list 1 to the pool of global addresses named MY POOL.

You can list all NAT translations using the show ip nat translations command:

```
R1#show ip nat translations
Pro   Inside global      Inside local       Outside local      Outside global
tcp   155.4.12.1:1025    10.0.0.100:1025    155.4.12.5:80      155.4.12.5:80
```

In the picture above you can see that the translation has been made between the Host A's private IP address (Inside local, 10.0.0.100) to the first available public IP address from the pool (Inside global, 155.4.12.1).

> NOTE
>
> You can remove all NAT translations from the table by using the clear ip nat translation * command.

Port Address Translation (PAT) configuration

With **Port Address Translation (PAT),** a single public IP address is used for all internal private IP addresses, but a different port is assigned to each private IP address. This type of NAT is also known as NAT Overload and is the typical form of NAT used in today's networks. It is even supported by most consumer-grade routers.

PAT allows you to support many hosts with only few public IP addresses. It works by creating dynamic NAT mapping, in which a global (public) IP address and a unique port number are selected. The router keeps a NAT table entry for every unique combination of the private IP address and port, with translation to the global address and a unique port number.

We will use the following example network to explain the benefits of using PAT:

```
                10.0.0.100/24
```

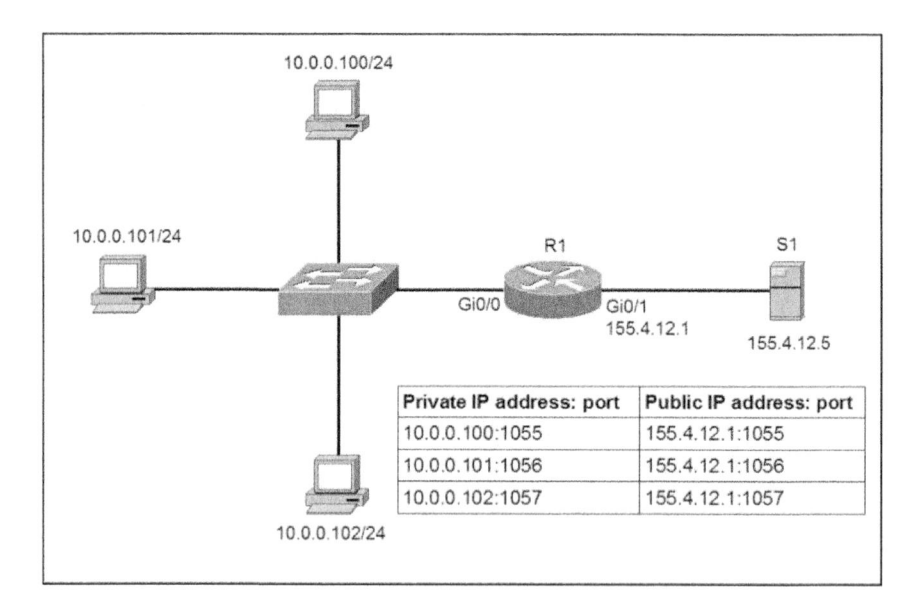

Private IP address: port	Public IP address: port
10.0.0.100:1055	155.4.12.1:1055
10.0.0.101:1056	155.4.12.1:1056
10.0.0.102:1057	155.4.12.1:1057

As you can see in the picture above, PAT uses unique source port numbers on the inside global (public) IP address to distinguish between translations. For example, if the host with the IP address of 10.0.0.101 wants to access the server S1 on the Internet, the host's private IP address will be translated by R1 to 155.4.12.1:1056 and the request will be sent to S1. S1 will respond to 155.4.12.1:1056. R1 will receive that response, look up in its NAT translation table, and forward the request to the host.

To configure PAT, the following commands are required:

- configure the router's inside interface using the ip nat inside command.
- configure the router's outside interface using the ip nat outside command.
- configure an access list that includes a list of the inside source addresses that should be translated.
- enable PAT with the ip nat inside source list ACL_NUMBER interface TYPE overload global configuration command.

Here is how we would configure PAT for the network picture above.

First, we will define the outside and inside interfaces on R1:

```
R1(config)#int Gi0/0
R1(config-if)#ip nat inside
R1(config-if)#int Gi0/1
R1(config-if)#ip nat outside
```

Next, we will define an access list that will include all private IP addresses we would like to translate:

```
R1(config-if)#access-list 1 permit 10.0.0.0 0.0.0.255
```

The access list defined above includes all IP addresses from the 10.0.0.0 – 10.0.0.255 range.

Now we need to enable NAT and refer to the ACL created in the previous step and to the interface whose IP address will be used for translations:

```
R1(config)#ip nat inside source list 1 interface Gi0/1 overload
```

To verify the NAT translations, we can use the show ip nat translations command after hosts request a web resource from S1:

```
R1#show ip nat translations
Pro Inside global Inside local Outside local Outside global
tcp 155.4.12.1:1024 10.0.0.100:1025 155.4.12.5:80 155.4.12.5:80
tcp 155.4.12.1:1025 10.0.0.101:1025 155.4.12.5:80 155.4.12.5:80
tcp 155.4.12.1:1026 10.0.0.102:1025 155.4.12.5:80 155.4.12.5:80
```

PART X: IPv6

What is IPv6?

IPv6 is the newest version of the IP protocol. IPv6 was developed to overcome many deficiencies of IPv4, most notably the problem of IPv4 address exhaustion. Unlike IPv4, which has only about 4.3 billion (2 raised to power 32) available addresses, IPv6 allows for 3.4 × 10 raised to power 38 addresses.

IPv6 features

Here is a list of the most important features of IPv6:

- Large address space: IPv6 uses 128-bit addresses, which means that for each person on the Earth there are 48,000,000,000,000,000,000,000,000,000 addresses!
- Enhanced security: IPSec (Internet Protocol Security) is built into IPv6 as part of the protocol. This means that two devices can dynamically create a secure tunnel without user intervention.
- Header improvements: the packed header used in IPv6 is simpler than the one used in IPv4. The IPv6 header is not protected by a checksum so routers do not need to calculate a checksum for every packet.
- No need for NAT: since every device has a globally unique IPv6 address, there is no need for NAT.
- Stateless address autoconfiguration: IPv6 devices can automatically configure themselves with an IPv6 address.

IPv6 address format

Unlike IPv4, which uses a dotted-decimal format with each byte ranges from 0 to 255, IPv6 uses eight groups of four hexadecimal digits separated by colons. For example, this is a valid IPv6 address:

2340:0023:AABA:0A01:0055:5054:9ABC:ABB0

If you don't know how to convert hexadecimal number to binary, here is a table that will help you do the conversion:

Hex	Binary	Hex	Binary
0	0000	8	1000
1	0001	9	1001
2	0010	A	1010
3	0011	B	1011
4	0100	C	1100
5	0101	D	1101
6	0110	E	1110
7	0111	F	1111

IPv6 address shortening

The IPv6 address given above looks daunting, right? Well, there are two conventions that can help you shorten what must be typed for an IP address:

1. A leading zero can be omitted

For example, the address listed above (2340:0023:AABA:0A01:0055:5054:9ABC:ABB0) can be shortened to 2340:23:AABA:A01:55:5054:9ABC:ABB0

2. Successive fields of zeroes can be represented as two colons (::)

For example, **2340:0000:0000:0000:0455:0000:AAAB:1121** can be written as **2340::0455:0000:AAAB:1121**

> NOTE
>
> You can shorten an address this way only for one such occurrence. The reason is obvious — if you had more than occurrence of double colon you wouldn't know how many sets of zeroes were being omitted from each part.

Here is a couple of more examples that can help you grasp the concept of IPv6 address shortening:

Long version: **1454:0045:0000:0000:4140:0141:0055:ABBB**

Shortened version: **1454:45::4140:141:55:ABBB**

Long version: **0000:0000:0001:AAAA:BBBC:A222:BBBA:0001**

Shortened version: **::1:AAAA:BBBC:A222:BBBA:1**

Types of IPv6 addresses

Three categories of IPv6 addresses exist:

- ❖ **Unicast** – represents a single interface. Packets addressed to a unicast address are delivered to a single interface.
- ❖ **Anycast** – identifies one or more interfaces. For example, servers that support the same function can use the same unicast IP address. Packets sent to that IP address are forwarded to the nearest server. Anycast addresses are used for load-balancing. Known as "one-to-nearest" address.
- ❖ **Multicast** – represent a dynamic group of hosts. Packets sent to this address are delivered to many interfaces. Multicast addresses in IPv6 have a similar purpose as their counterparts in IPv4.

> NOTE
>
> IPv6 doesn't use the broadcast method. It has been replaced with anycast and multicast addresses.

IPv6 unicast addresses

Unicast addresses represent a single interface. Packets addressed to a unicast address will be delivered to a specific network interface.

There are three types of IPv6 unicast addresses:

- ❖ **global unicast** – similar to IPv4 public IP addresses. These addresses are assigned by the IANA and used on public networks. They have a prefix of 2000::/3, (all the addresses that begin with binary 001).
- ❖ **unique local** – similar to IPv4 private addresses. They are used in private networks and aren't routable on the Internet. These addresses have a prefix of FD00::/8.

link local – these addresses are used for sending packets over the local subnet. Routers do not forward packets with this addresses to other subnets. IPv6 requires a link-local address to be assigned to every network interface on which the IPv6 protocol is enabled. These addresses have a prefix of FE80::/10.

IPv6 global unicast addresses

IPv6 global addresses are similar to IPv4 public addresses. As the name implies, they are routable on the internet. Currently IANA has assigned only 2000::/3 addresses to the global pool.

A global IPv6 address consists of two parts:

- subnet ID – 64 bits long. Contains the site prefix (obtained from a Regional Internet Registry) and the subnet ID (subnets within the site).
- interface ID – 64 bits long, typically composed of a part of the MAC address of the interface.

Here is a graphical representation of the two parts of a global IPv6 address:

3 bits	45 bits	16 bits	64 bits
001	Global Routing Prefix	Subnet ID	Interface ID

IPv6 unique local addresses

Unique local IPv6 addresses have the similar function as IPv4 private addresses. They are not allocated by an address registry and are not meant to be routed outside their domain. Unique local IPv6 addresses begin with FD00::/8.

A unique local IPv6 address is constructed by appending a randomly generated 40-bit hexadecimal string to the FD00::/8 prefix. The subnet field and interface ID are created in the same way as with global IPv6 addresses.

A graphical representation of a unique local IPv6 address:

8 bits	40 bits	16 bits	64 bits
FD	Global ID	Subnet ID	Interface ID

NOTE

The original IPv6 RFCs defined a private address class called site local. This class has been deprecated and replaced with unique local addresses.

IPv6 link-local addresses

Link-local IPv6 addresses have a smaller scope as to how far they can travel: only within a network segment that a host is connected to. Routers will not forward packets destined to a link-local address to other links. A link-local IPv6 address must be assigned to every network interface on which the IPv6 protocol is enabled. A host can automatically derive its own link local IP address or the address can be manually configured.

Link-local addresses have a prefix of FE80::/10. They are mostly used for auto-address configuration and neighbor discovery.

Here is a graphical representation of a link local IPv6 address:

64 bits	64 bits
FE80:0000:0000:0000	Interface ID

IPv6 multicast addresses

Here is a graphical representation of the IPv6 multicast packet:

8 bits	4 bits	4 bits	112 bits
FF	Flags	Scope	Group ID

IPv6 multicast addresses start with FF00::/8. After the first 8 bits there are 4 bits which represent the flag fields that indicate the nature of specific multicast addresses. Next 4 bits indicate the scope of the IPv6 network for which the multicast traffic is intended. Routers use the scope field to determine whether multicast traffic can be forwarded. The remaining 112 bits of the address make up the multicast Group ID.

Some of the possible scope values are:

For example, the addresses that begin with FF02::/16 are multicast addresses intended to stay on the local link.

The following table lists of some of the most common link local multicast addresses:

Purpose	Address
All nodes on the link	FF02::1
All routers on the link	FF02::2
OSPF	FF02::5, FF02::6
RIP-2	FF02::9
EIGRP	FF02::A

IPv6 address prefixes

Type of Address	Prefix (hex)
Global	2000::/3
Unique Local	FD00::/8
Link-local	FE80::/10
Multicast	FF00::/8

IPv6 interface identifier

For example, if the MAC address of a network card is 00:BB:CC:DD:11:22 the interface ID would be 02BBCCFFFEDD1122.

Why is that so?

118

Well, first we need to flip the seventh bit from 0 to 1. MAC addresses are in hex format. The binary format of the MAC address looks like this:

hex 00BBCCDD1122
binary 0000 0000 1011 1011 1100 1100 1101 1101 0001 0001 0010 0010

We need to flip the seventh bit:

binary 0000 0010 1011 1011 1100 1100 1101 1101 0001 0001 0010 0010

Now we have this address in hex:

hex 02BBCCDD1122

Next, we need to insert FFFE in the middle of the address listed above:

hex 02BBCCFFFEDD1122

So, the interface ID is now 02BB:CCFF:FEDD:1122.

Another example, this time with the MAC address of 00000C432A35.

binary: 0000 0010 0000 0000 0000 1100 0100 0011 0010 1010 0011 0101

hex: 02000C432A35

IPv6 transition options

IPv4 and IPv6 networks are not interoperable and the number of devices that use IPv4 number is still large. Some of these devices do not support IPv6 at all, so the migration process is necessary since IPv4 and IPv6 will likely coexist for some time.

Many transition mechanisms have been proposes.

NOTE

Some methods of the IPv4-IPV6 transition have been deprecated, but they are still mentioned in the older books. Some of these methods are NAT-PT and NAPT-PT.

IPv6 routing protocols

Like IPv4, IPv6 also supports routing protocols that enable routers to exchange information about connected networks. IPv6 routing protocols can be internal (RIPng, EIGRP for IPv6…) and external (BGP).

As with IPv4, IPv6 routing protocols can be distance vector and link-state. An example of a distance vector protocol is RIPng with hop count as the metric. An example of a link-state routing protocol is OSPF with cost as the metric.

IPv6 supports the following routing protocols:

- RIPng (RIP New Generation)
- OSPFv3
- EIGRP for IPv6
- IS-IS for IPv6
- MP-BGP4 (Multiprotocol BGP-4)

How to configure IPv6

Cisco routers do not have IPv6 routing enabled by default. To configure IPv6 on a Cisco router, you need to do two things:

1. enable IPv6 routing on a Cisco router using the ipv6 unicast-routing global configuration command. This command globally enables IPv6 and must be the first command executed on the router.

2. configure the IPv6 global unicast address on an interface using the ipv6 address address/prefix-length [eui-64] command. If you omit the eui-64 parameter, you will need to configure the entire address manually. After you enter this command, the link local address will be automatically derived.

Here is an IPv6 configuration example:

```
R1(config)#ipv6 unicast-routing
R1(config)#int G0/0
R1(config-if)#ipv6 address 2001:0BB9:AABB:1234::/64 eui-64
```

We can verify that the IPv6 address has been configured by using the show ipv6 interface G0/0 command:

```
R1#show ipv6 interface G0/0
GigabitEthernet0/0 is up, line protocol is up
 IPv6 is enabled, link-local address is FE80::201:42FF:FE65:3E01
 No Virtual link-local address(es):
 Global unicast address(es):
   2001:BB9:AABB:1234:201:42FF:FE65:3E01, subnet is
2001:BB9:AABB:1234::/64 [EUI]
 Joined group address(es):
   FF02::1
   FF02::2
   FF02::1:FF65:3E01
 MTU is 1500 bytes
 ....
```

From the output above we can verify two things:

120

1. the link local IPv6 address has been automatically configured. Link local IP addresses begin with FE80::/10 and the interface ID is used for the rest of the address. Because the MAC address of the interface is 00:01:42:65:3E01, the calculated address is FE80::201:42FF:FE65:3E01.

2. the global IPv6 address has been created using the modified EUI-64 method. Remember that IPv6 global addresses begin with 2000::/3. So in our case, the IPv6 global address is 2001:BB9:AABB:1234:201:42FF:FE65:3E01.

We will also create an IPv6 address on another router. This time we will enter the whole address:

```
R2(config-if)#ipv6 address 2001:0BB9:AABB:1234:1111:2222:3333:4444/64
```

Notice that the IPv6 address is in the same subnet as the one configured on R1 (2001:0BB9:AABB:1234/64). We can test the connectivity between the devices using ping for IPv6:

```
R1#ping ipv6 2001:0BB9:AABB:1234:1111:2222:3333:4444
Type escape sequence to abort.
Sending 5, 100-byte ICMP Echos to 2001:0BB9:AABB:1234:1111:2222:3333:4444,
timeout is 2 seconds:
!!!!!
Success rate is 100 percent (5/5), round-trip min/avg/max = 0/0/0 ms
```

As you can see from the output above, the devices can communicate with each other.

RIPng

RIPng is an extension of RIP developed for support of IPv6. Here are some of its features:

- just like RIP for IPv4, it uses hop count as the metric
- sends updates every 30 seconds
- RIPng messages use the UDP port 521 and the multicast address of FF02::9

The configuration of RIPng is requires at least two steps:

Here is an example:

```
Router(config)#ipv6 router rip router_1
Router(config-rtr)#int fa0/1
Router(config-if)#ipv6 rip router_1 enable
```

We have done a similar configuration on the second router. To verify that routers are indeed exchanging route information using RIPng we can use the show ipv6 route command:

```
Router#show ipv6 route
IPv6 Routing Table - 4 entries
Codes: C - Connected, L - Local, S - Static, R - RIP, B - BGP
       U - Per-user Static route, M - MIPv6
       I1 - ISIS L1, I2 - ISIS L2, IA - ISIS interarea, IS - ISIS summary
       O - OSPF intra, OI - OSPF inter, OE1 - OSPF ext 1, OE2 - OSPF ext 2
       ON1 - OSPF NSSA ext 1, ON2 - OSPF NSSA ext 2
       D - EIGRP, EX - EIGRP external
C   2001:BB9:AABB:1234::/64 [0/0]
     via ::, FastEthernet0/1
L   2001:BB9:AABB:1234:201:64FF:FE8D:AC02/128 [0/0]
     via ::, FastEthernet0/1
R   2001:BBBB:CCCC:DDDD::/64 [120/2]
     via FE80::20B:BEFF:FEDD:C902, FastEthernet0/1
L   FF00::/8 [0/0]
     via ::, Null0
```

In the picture above, we can see that the router has received a route to the network 2001:BBBB:CCCC:DDDD::/64.

Differences between IPv4 and IPv6

The following table summarizes the major differences between IPv4 and IPv6:

Feature	IPv4	IPv6
Address length	32 bits	128 bits
Address representation	4 decimal numbers from 0-255 separated by periods	8 groups of 4 hexadecimal digits separated by colons
Address types	Unicast, multicast, broadcast	Unicast, multicast, anycast
Packet header	20 bytes long	40 bytes long, but simpler than IPv4 header
Configuration	Manual, DHCP	Manual, DHCP, auto-configuration built-in
IPSec support	Optional	Built-in

PART XI: STP and RSTP

What is STP?

Spanning Tree Protocol (STP) is a network protocol designed to prevent layer 2 loops. It is standardized as IEEE 802.D protocol. STP blocks some ports on switches with redundant links to prevent broadcast storms and ensure loop-free topology. With STP in place, you can have redundant links between switches in order to provide redundancy.

To better understand the importance of STP and how STP prevents broadcast storms on a network with redundant links, consider the following example:

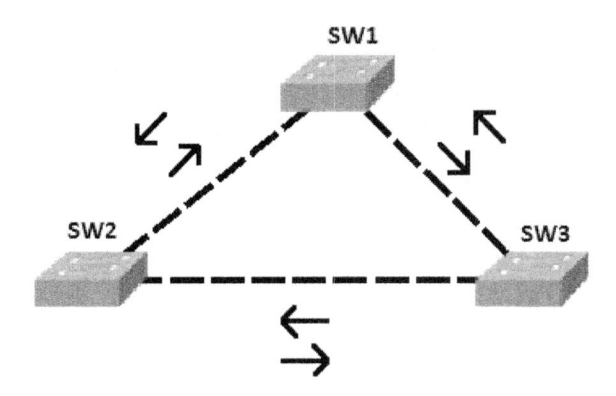

SW1 sends a broadcast frame to SW2 and SW3. Both switches receive the frame and forward the frame out every port, except the port the frame was received on. So SW2 forwards the frame to SW3. SW3 receives that frame, and forwards it to SW1. SW1 then again forwards the frame to SW2! The same thing also happens in the opposite direction. Without STP in place, these frames would loop forever. STP prevents loops by placing one of the switch ports in blocking state.

So, our topology above could look like this:

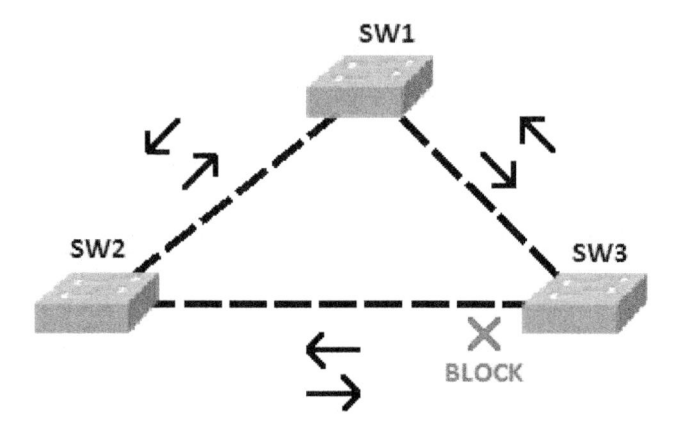

In the topology above, STP has placed one port on SW3 in the blocking state. That port will no longer process any frames except the STP messages. If SW3 receives a broadcast frame from SW1, it will not forward it out the port connected to SW2.

> NOTE
>
> STP enables layer 2 redundancy. In the example above, if the link between SW3 and SW1 fails, STP would converge and unblock the port on SW3.

How STP works

STP uses the Spanning-Tree Algorithm (SPA) to create a topology database of the network. To prevent loops, SPA places some interfaces in forwarding state and other interfaces in blocking state. How does STP decides in which state the port will be placed? A couple of criteria exist:

> NOTE
>
> STP considers only working interfaces – shutdown interfaces or interfaces without the cable installed are placed in an STP disabled state.

An example will help you understand the concept:

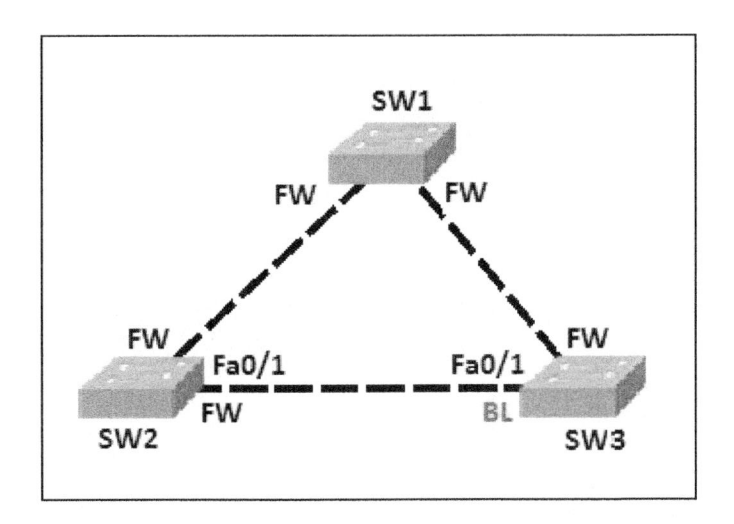

Let's say that SW1 is elected as the root switch. All ports on SW1 are placed into forwarding state. SW2 and SW3 choose ports with the lowest cost to reach the root switch to be the root ports. These ports are also placed in forwarding state. On the shared Ethernet segment between SW2 and SW3, port Fa0/1 on SW2 has the lowest cost to reach the root switch. This port is placed in forwarding state. To prevent loops, port Fa0/1 on SW3 is placed in blocking state.

NOTE

A switch with the lowest switch ID will become the root switch. A switch ID consists of two components: the switch's priority (by default 32,768 on Cisco switches) and the switch's MAC address.

BPDU (Bridge Protocol Data Unit)

BPDUs are messages used by switches to share STP information with each other in order to elect a root switch and detect loops. The most common messages are Hello BPDUs which include the following information:

- root switch ID
- sender's switch ID
- sender's root cost
- Hello, Max Age, and forward delay timers

Electing the Root Switch in STP

The STP process works by default on Cisco switches and begins with the root switch election. The election is based on the bridge IDs (BIDs) sent in the BPDUs. Each switch that participates in STP will have an 8-byte switch ID that comprises of the following fields:

- 2-byte priority field – by default, all switches have the priority of 32768. This value can be changed using configuration commands.
- 6-byte system ID – a value based on the MAC address of each switch.

A switch with the lowest BID will become a root switch, with lower number meaning better priority.

Consider the following example:

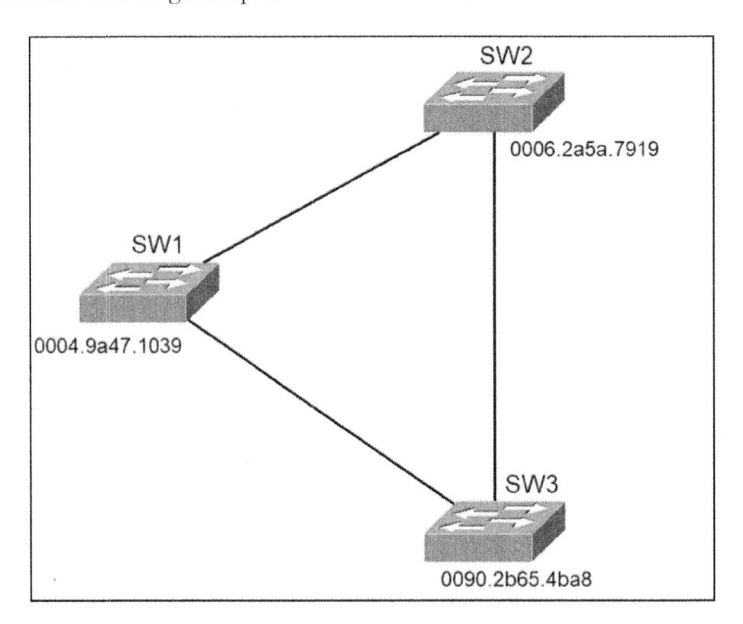

```
                            SW2
                            0006.2a5a.7919

         SW1

         0004.9a47.1039

                            SW3
                            0090.2b65.4ba8
```

As mentioned above, the switch with the lower BID wins. Since by default all switches have the BID priority of 32768, the second comparison must be made – the lowest MAC address. In our example SW1 has the lowest MAC address and becomes the root switch.

NOTE

For simplicity, all ports on switches in the example above are assigned to VLAN 1. Also, note that STA adds the VLAN number to the priority value, so all switches actually have the BID priority of 32,769.

To influence the election process, you can change the BID priority to a lower value on a switch you would like to become root. This can be done using the following command:

(config)#spanning-tree vlan ID priority VALUE

The priority must be in increments of 4096, so if you choose any other value, you will get an error and possible values listed:

126

(config)#spanning-tree vlan 1 priority 224
% Bridge Priority must be in increments of 4096.
% Allowed values are:
0 4096 8192 12288 16384 20480 24576 28672
32768 36864 40960 45056 49152 53248 57344 61440
(config)#spanning-tree vlan 1 priority 4096

Selecting STP root port

As we've mentioned before, all working interfaces on the root switch are placed in forwarding state. All other switches (called non root switches) determine the best path to get to the root switch and the port used to reach the root switch is placed in forwarding state. The best path is the one with the lowest cost to reach the root switch. The cost is calculated by adding the individual port costs along the path from the switch to the root.

Take a look the following example:

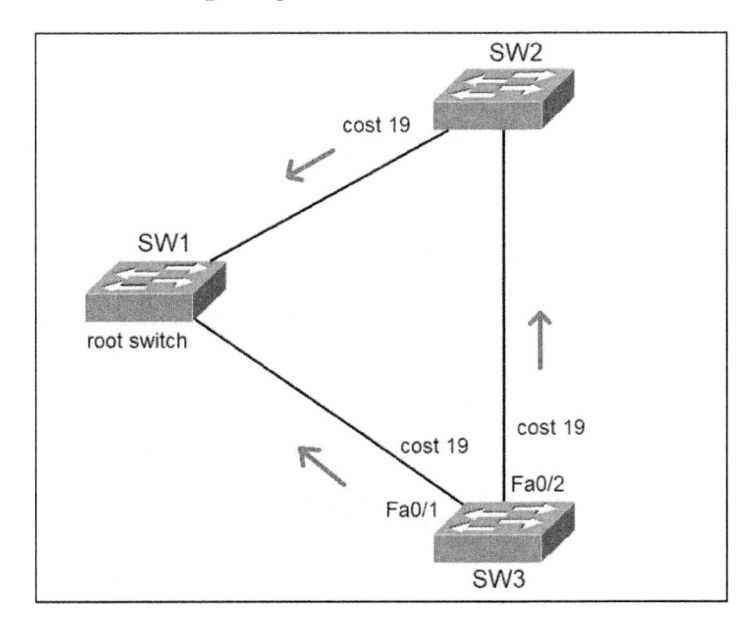

SW1 has won the election process and is the root switch. Consider the SW3's perspective for choosing its root port. Two paths are available to reach the root switch, one direct path over Fa0/1 and the other going out Fa0/2 and through SW2. The direct path has a cost of 19, while the indirect path has the cost of 38 (19+19). That is why Fa0/1 will become the root port on SW3.

In case the best root cost ties for two or more paths, the following tiebreakers are applied:

The default port cost is defined by the operating speed of the interface:

Speed	Cost
10 Mbps	100
100 Mbps	19
1 Gbps	4
10 Gbps	2

You can override the default value on the per-interface basis using the following command:

(config-if)#spanning-tree cost VALUE

Selecting STP designated port (DP)

We've already learned that, on the shared Ethernet segments, the switch with the best path to reach the root switch is placed in forwarding state. That switch is called the designated switch and its port is known as the designated port. In order to avoid loops, the non-designated port on the other end of the link is placed in blocking state.

The designated switch is determined based on the following criteria:

Consider the following example:

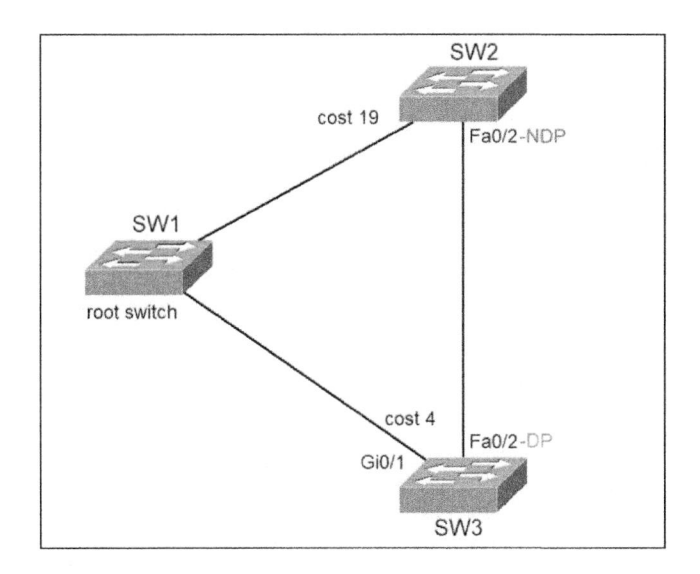

SW1 has the lowest BID and has been selected as the root switch. SW2 and SW3 have then determined their own root port to reach the root switch. On the shared network segment between SW2 and SW3 a designated port needs to be selected. Because SW3 has the lower cost to reach the root switch (4<19), its Fa0/2 port will be the designated port for the segment. The Fa0/2 port on SW2 will be placed in blocking state.

> NOTE
>
> If the link between SW1 and SW3 fails, STP will converge and the Fa0/2 port on SW2 will be placed in the forwarding state.

What is RSTP?

RSTP (Rapid Spanning Tree Protocol) is an evolution of STP. It was originally introduced as IEEE 802.1w standard and in 2004 IEEE decided to replace STP with RSTP in 802.1D standard. Finally, in 2011, in the IEEE decided to move all the RSTP details into 802.1Q standard.

RSTP is backwards-compatible with STP and there are many similarities between the two protocols, such as:

- ❖ the root switch is elected using the same set of rules in both protocols
- ❖ root ports are selected with the same rules, as well as designated port on LAN segments
- ❖ both STP and RSTP place each port in either forwarding or blocking state. The blocking state in RSTP is called the discarding state.

However, there are differences between STP and RSTP:

- RSTP enables faster convergence times than STP (usually within just a couple of seconds)
- STP ports states listening, blocking, and disabled are merged into a single state in RSTP – the discarding state
- STP features two port types – root and designated port. RSTP adds two additional port types – alternate and backup port.

With STP, the root switch generates and sends Hellos to all other switches, which are then relayed by the non-root switches. With RSTP, each switch can generate its own Hellos. Consider the following network topology with RSTP turned on:

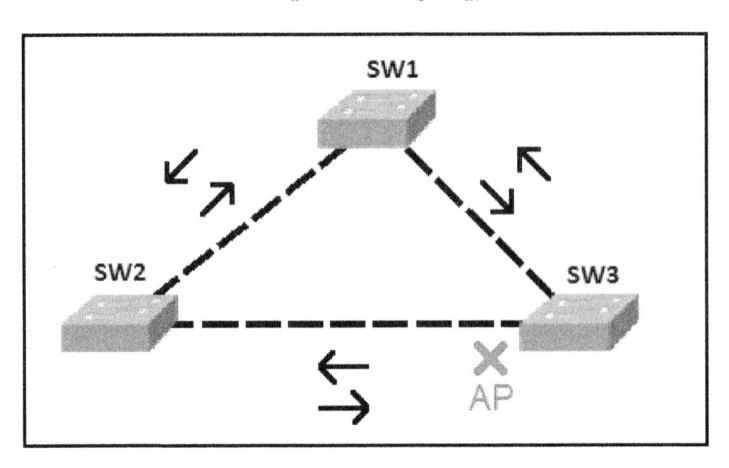

In order to avoid loops, RSTP has placed one port on SW3 in the alternate state. This port will not process or forward any frames except the RSTP messages. However, if the root port on SW3 fails, the alternate port will rapidly become the root port and start forwarding frames.

How RSTP works

Just like STP, RSTP creates a topology database of the network. To prevent loops, some interfaces on switches are placed in forwarding state and other interfaces in discarding state. How does RSTP decides in which state the port will be placed? A couple of criteria exist:

> NOTE
>
> RSTP is backwards-compatible with STP and they both can be used in the same network.

Consider the following example:

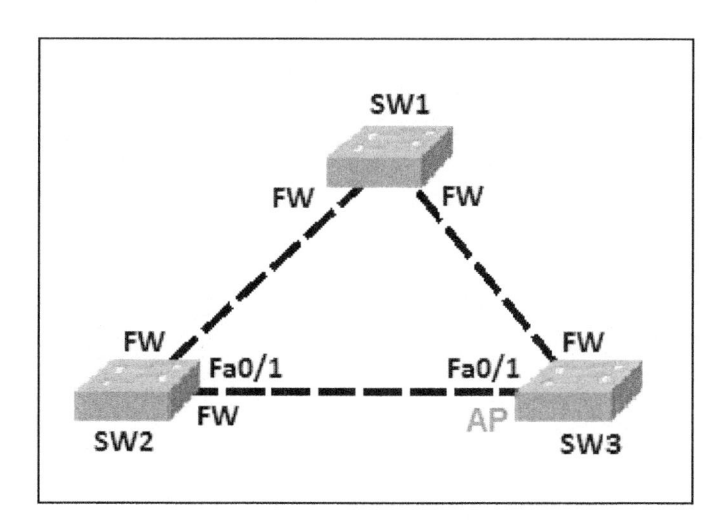

Let's say that SW1 is elected as the root switch. All ports on SW1 are placed in forwarding state. SW2 and SW3 choose ports with the lowest cost to reach the root switch to be the root ports. These ports are also placed in forwarding state. On the shared Ethernet segment between SW2 and SW3, port Fa0/1 on SW2 has the lowest cost to reach the root switch. This port is placed in forwarding state. To prevent loops, port Fa0/1 on SW3 is placed in discarding state. If the root port on SW3 fails, this alternate port will quickly take over and become the root port.

> NOTE
>
> RSTP also introduces a concept of backup port. This port serves as a replacement for the designated port inside the same collision domain. This can only occur when using hubs in your network.

Configuring RSTP

Most newer Cisco switches use RSTP by default. RSTP prevents frame looping out of the box and no additional configuration is necessary. To check whether a switch runs RSTP, the show spanning-tree command is used:

```
SW1#show spanning-tree
VLAN0001
  Spanning tree enabled protocol rstp
  Root ID    Priority    32769
             Address     0004.9A47.1039
             This bridge is the root
             Hello Time  2 sec  Max Age 20 sec  Forward Delay 15 sec
  Bridge ID  Priority    32769  (priority 32768 sys-id-ext 1)
             Address     0004.9A47.1039
             Hello Time  2 sec  Max Age 20 sec  Forward Delay 15 sec
```

```
           Aging Time  20
Interface      Role Sts Cost     Prio.Nbr Type
---------------- ---- --- --------- -------- ------------------------------
Fa0/3          Desg FWD 19       128.3   P2p
Fa0/2          Desg FWD 19       128.2   P2p
```

If RSTP is not being used, the following command will enable it:

```
SW1(config)#spanning-tree mode rapid-pvst
```

What are ACLs?

For example on how ACLs are used, consider the following network topology:

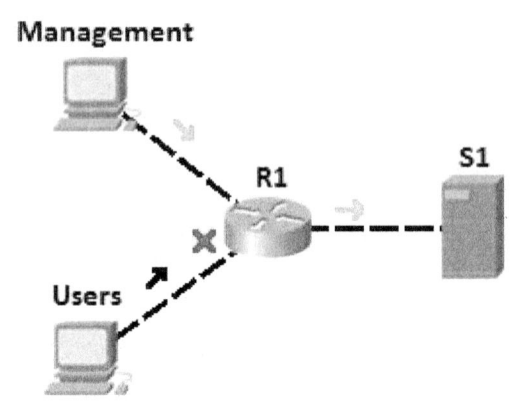

Let's say that server S1 holds some important documents that need to be available only to the company's management. We could configure an access list on R1 to enable access to S1 only to users from the management network. All other traffic going to S1 will be blocked. This way, we can ensure that only authorized user can access the sensitive files on S1.

Types of ACLs

There are two types of access lists:

The following example describes the way in which standard access lists can be used.

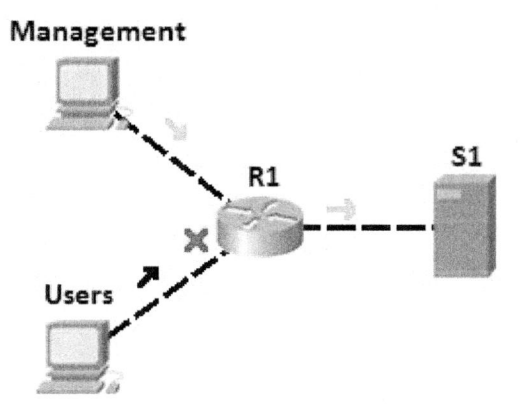

Let's say that server S1 holds some important documents that need to be available only to company's management. We could configure an access list on R1 to enable access to S1 only to users from the management network. All other traffic going to S1 will be blocked. This way, we can ensure that only authorized user can access sensitive files on S1.

To demonstrate the usefulness of extended ACLs, we will use the following example.

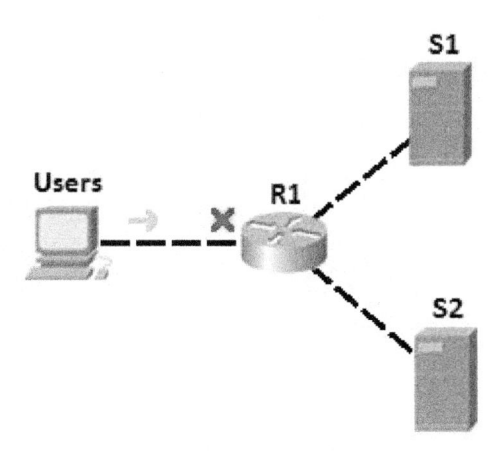

133

In the example network above, we have used the standard access list to prevent all users to access server S1. But, with that configuration, we have also disable access to S2! To be more specific, we can use extended access lists. Let's say that we need to prevent users from accessing server S1. We could place an extended access list on R1 to prevent users only from accessing S1 (we would use an access list to filter the traffic according to the destination IP address). That way, no other traffic is forbidden, and users can still access the other server, S2:

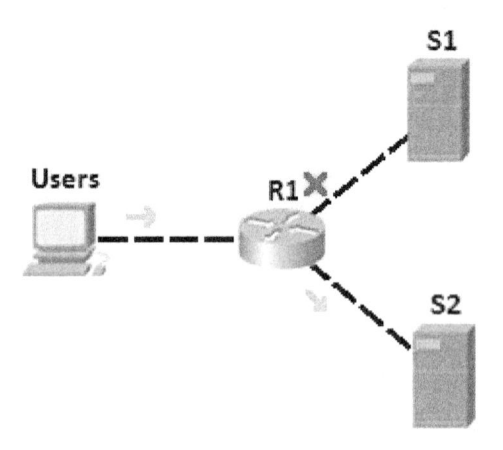

Configuring standard ACLs

To create a standard access list on a Cisco router, the following command is used from the router's global configuration mode:

R1(config)# access-list ACL_NUMBER permit|deny IP_ADDRESS WILDCARD_MASK

NOTE

ACL number for the standard ACLs has to be between 1–99 and 1300–1999.

You can also use the host keyword to specify the host you want to permit or deny:

R1(config)# access-list ACL_NUMBER permit|deny host IP_ADDRESS

Once the access list is created, it needs to be applied to an interface. You do that by using the ip access-group ACL_NUMBER in|out interface subcommand. in and out keywords specify in which direction you are activating the ACL. in means that ACL is applied to the traffic coming into the interface, while the out keyword means that the ACL is applied to the traffic leaving the interface.

Consider the following network topology:

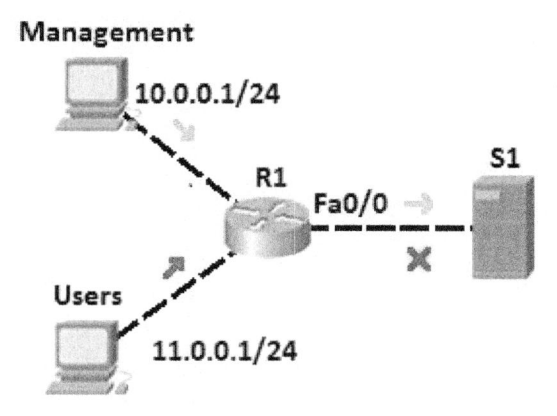

Management
10.0.0.1/24

R1
Fa0/0

S1

Users
11.0.0.1/24

We want to allow traffic from the management LAN to the server S1. First, we need to write an ACL to permit traffic from LAN 10.0.0.0/24 to S1. We can use the following command on R1:

R1(config)#access-list 1 permit 10.0.0.0 0.0.0.255

The command above permits traffic from all IP addresses that begin with 10.0.0. We could also target the specific host by using the host keyword:

R1(config)#access-list 1 permit host 10.0.0.1

The command above permits traffic only from the host with the IP address of 10.0.0.1.

Next, we will deny traffic from the Users LAN (11.0.0.0/24):

R1(config)#access-list 1 deny 11.0.0.0 0.0.0.255

Next, we need to apply the access list to an interface. It is recommended to place the standard access lists as close to the destination as possible. In our case, this is the Fa0/0 interface on R1. Since we want to evaluate all packets trying to exit out Fa0/0, we will specify the outbound direction with the out keyword:

R1(config-if)#ip access-group 1 out

> **NOTE**
>
> At the end of each ACL there is an implicit deny all statement. This means that all traffic not specified in earlier ACL statements will be forbidden, so the second ACL statement (access-list 1 deny 11.0.0.0 0.0.0.255) wasn't even necessary.

Configuring extended ACLs

To be more precise when matching a certain network traffic, extended access lists are used. Extended access lists are more difficult to configure and require more processor time than the standard access lists, but they enable a much more granular level of control.

With extended access lists, you can evaluate additional packet information, such as:

- source and destination IP address
- type of TCP/IP protocol (TCP, UDP, IP…)
- source and destination port numbers

Two steps are required to configure an extended access list:

1. configure an extended access list using the following command:

> (config) access list NUMBER permit|deny IP_PROTOCOL SOURCE_ADDRESS WILDCARD_MASK [PROTOCOL_INFORMATION] DESTINATION_ADDRESS WILDCARD_MASK PROTOCOL_INFORMATION

2. apply an access list to an interface using the following command:

> (config) ip access-group ACL_NUMBER in | out

> **NOTE**
>
> Extended access lists numbers are in ranges from 100 to 199 and from 2000 to 2699. You should always place extended ACLs as close to the source of the packets that are being evaluated as possible.

To better understand the concept of extended access lists, consider the following example:

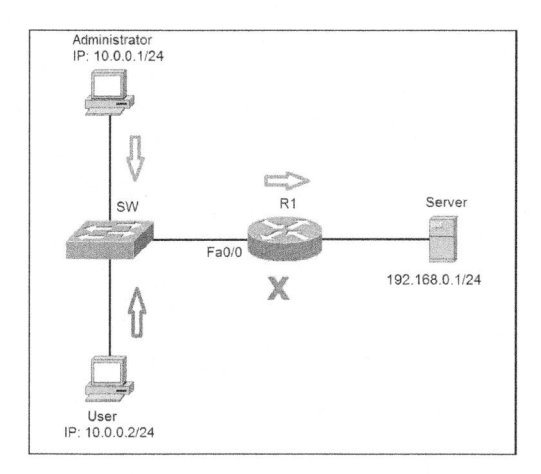

We want to enable the administrator's workstation (10.0.0.1/24) unrestricted access to Server (192.168.0.1/24). We will also deny any type of access to Server from the user's workstation (10.0.0.2/24).

First, we'll create a statement that will permit the administrator's workstation access to Server:

```
R1(config)#access-list 100 permit ip 10.0.0.1 0.0.0.0 192.168.0.1 0.0.0.0
```

Next, we need to create a statement that will deny the user's workstation access to Server:

```
R1(config)#access-list 100 deny ip 10.0.0.2 0.0.0.0 192.168.0.1 0.0.0.0
```

Lastly, we need to apply the access list to the Fa0/0 interface on R1:

```
R1(config)#int fa0/0
R1(config-if)#ip access-group 100 in
```

This will force the router to evaluate all packets entering Fa0/0. If the administrator tries to access Server, the traffic will be allowed, because of the first statement. However, if User tries to access Server, the traffic will be forbidden because of the second ACL statement.

> NOTE
>
> At the end of each access list there is an explicit deny all statement, so the second ACL statement wasn't really necessary. After applying an access list, every traffic not explicitly permitted will be denied.

What if we need to allow traffic to Server only for certain services? For example, let's say that Server was a web server and users should be able to access the web pages stored on it. We can allow traffic to Server only to certain ports (in this case, port 80), and deny any other type of traffic. Consider the following example:

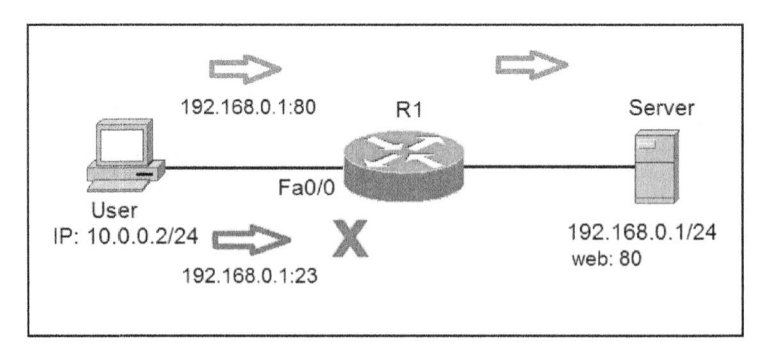

On the right side, we have a Server that serves as a web server, listening on port 80. We need to permit User to access web sites on S1 (port 80), but we also need to deny other type of access.

First, we need to allow traffic from User to the Server port of 80. We can do that using the following command:

```
R1(config)#access-list 100 permit tcp 10.0.0.2 0.0.0.0 192.168.0.1 0.0.0.0 eq 80
```

By using the tcp keyword, we can filter packets by the source and destination ports. In the example above, we have permitted traffic from 10.0.0.2 (User's workstation) to 192.168.0.1 (Server) on port 80. The last part of the statement, eq 80, specifies the destination port of 80.

Since at the end of each access list there is an implicit deny all statement, we don't need to define any more statement. After applying an access list, every traffic not originating from 10.0.0.2 and going to 192.168.0.1, port 80 will be denied.

We need to apply the access list to the interface:

```
R1(config)#int fa0/0
R1(config-if)#ip access-group 100 in
```

We can verify whether our configuration was successful by trying to access Server from the User's workstation using different methods. For example, the ping will fail:

```
PC>ping 192.168.0.1

Pinging 192.168.0.1 with 32 bytes of data:

Reply from 10.0.0.100: Destination host unreachable.
Reply from 10.0.0.100: Destination host unreachable.
```

Telnetting to the port 21 will fail:

```
PC>telnet 192.168.0.1 21
Trying 192.168.0.1 ...
% Connection timed out; remote host not responding
```

However, we will be able to access Server on port 80 using our browser:

Web Browser   X

< > URL http://192.168.0.1   Go   Stop

Cisco Packet Tracer

Welcome to Cisco Packet Tracer. Opening doors to new opportunities. Mind Wide Open.

Quick Links:
A small page
Copyrights
Image page
Image

Configuring named ACLs

Just like the numbered ACLs we've used so far, named ACLs allow you to filter network traffic according to various criteria. However, they have the following benefits over numbered ACLs:

- ❖ an ALC can be assigned a meaningful name (e.g. filter_traffic_to_server)
- ❖ ACL subcommands are used in the ACL configuration mode, and not in the global configuration mode as with numbered ACLs
- ❖ you can reorder statements in a named access list using sequence numbers

> NOTE
>
> Just like numbered ACLs, named ACLs can be of two types: standard and extended.

The named ACL name and type is defined using the following syntax:

(config) ip access-list STANDARD|EXTENDED NAME

The command above moves you to the ACL configuration mode, where you can configure the permit and deny statements. Just like with numbered ACLs, named ACLs ends with the implicit deny statement, so any traffic not explicitly permitted will be forbidden.

We will use the following network in our configuration example:

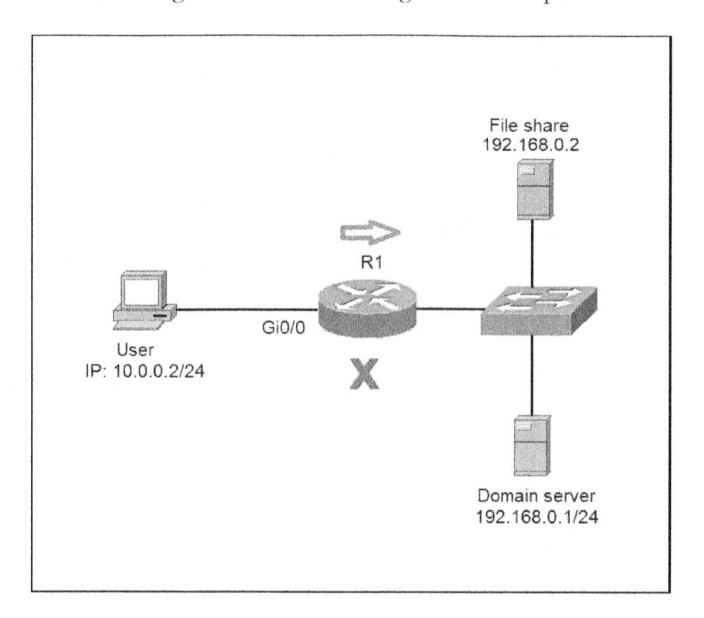

[Network diagram: User (IP: 10.0.0.2/24) connected via Gi0/0 to R1 router, which connects to a switch. The switch connects to File share (192.168.0.2) and Domain server (192.168.0.1/24).]

We want to deny the user's workstation (10.0.0.2/24) any type of access to the Domain server (192.168.0.1/24). We also want to enable the user unrestricted access to the File share (192.168.0.2/24).

First, we will create and name our ACL:

R1(config)#ip access-list extended allow_traffic_fileshare

Once inside the ACL config mode, we need to create a statement that will deny the user's workstation access to the Domain server:

R1(config-ext-nacl)#20 deny ip 10.0.0.2 0.0.0.0 192.168.0.1 0.0.0.0

The number 20 represents the line in which we want to place this entry in the ACL. This allows us to reorder statements later if needed.

Now, we will execute a statement that will permit the workstation access to the File share:

R1(config-ext-nacl)#50 permit ip 10.0.0.2 0.0.0.0 192.168.0.2 0.0.0.0

Lastly, we need to apply the access list to the Gi0/0 interface on R1:

```
R1(config)#int Gi0/0
R1(config-if)#ip access-group allow_traffic_fileshare in
```

The commands above will force the router to evaluate all packets trying to enter Gi0/0. If the workstation tries to access the Domain server, the traffic will be forbidden because of the first ACL statement. However, if the user tries to access the File server, the traffic will be allowed, because of the second statement.

Our named ACL configuration looks like this:

```
R1#show ip access-lists
Extended IP access list allow_traffic_fileshare
    20 deny ip host 10.0.0.2 host 192.168.0.1
    50 permit ip host 10.0.0.2 host 192.168.0.2
```

Notice the sequence number at the beginning of each entry. If we need to stick a new entry between these two entries, we can do that by specifying a sequence number in the range between 20 and 50. If we don't specify the sequence number, the entry will be added to the bottom of the list.

We can use the ping command on the workstation to verify the traffic is being blocked properly:

```
C:\>ping 192.168.0.1
Pinging 192.168.0.1 with 32 bytes of data:
Reply from 10.0.0.1: Destination host unreachable.
Reply from 10.0.0.1: Destination host unreachable.
Reply from 10.0.0.1: Destination host unreachable.
Reply from 10.0.0.1: Destination host unreachable.
Ping statistics for 192.168.0.1:
    Packets: Sent = 4, Received = 0, Lost = 4 (100% loss),
C:\>
C:\>ping 192.168.0.2
Pinging 192.168.0.2 with 32 bytes of data:
Reply from 192.168.0.2: bytes=32 time<1ms TTL=127
Reply from 192.168.0.2: bytes=32 time<1ms TTL=127
Reply from 192.168.0.2: bytes=32 time<1ms TTL=127
Reply from 192.168.0.2: bytes=32 time<1ms TTL=127
Ping statistics for 192.168.0.2:
    Packets: Sent = 4, Received = 4, Lost = 0 (0% loss),
Approximate round trip times in milli-seconds:
    Minimum = 0ms, Maximum = 0ms, Average = 0ms
```

As you can see from the ping output above, the traffic is being filtered properly.

Printed in Great Britain
by Amazon